Sweeten The Deal

How to Spot and Avoid the Big Red Flags in Online Dating

For Janelle –
to avoiding Sweeting
anyone's deal!

Denham

Elizabeth Denham

Sweeten The Deal
Final Version ED 2

ISBN: 978-1508805168

Cover Design and artwork: Michael Ilaqua

www.cybertheorist.com

Photo credit Back cover: Deanie Sexton

Published by Intellect Publishing
www.IntellectPublishing.com

www.SweetenTheDeal.com

Dedicated to my husband who
was worth the wait
and to my children, all five.

Sweeten The Deal

Foreword

I originally began this book as a blog called, "You Can't Make This Shit Up" because, in my case, the truth was better than anything I could make up. I had so many off-the-wall dates that all of my friends told me I needed to start writing them down to share with the world. After all, everyone needs a good laugh, and anyone who has ever had a bad date can relate to some of the things I experienced.

The stories of these less-than-ideal dates may lead you to think that I would discourage online dating. Much to the contrary! I also had good dates, blah dates and dates that just went nowhere for no particular reason. I did not write about those. They are not funny. But all of my dates, good, bad, weird, scary or just downright perplexing, taught me something.

And that is what is at the heart of "Sweeten the Deal."

In writing this book, I discovered just how much I had learned about myself and about dating. I learned that dating is not about rejection, but about finding someone with whom you are compatible. It is about identifying what you want and what you don't. Learning about what you don't want is just as important as learning about what you do. Online dating offered me a way to date more easily and develop some knowledge about these dates before even meeting them. With three young children at home, who has time to go out?

So I hope that in the reading, you will find some laughs and some surprises, but mostly I hope you find that you learned something from my experience.

Cheers.

Sweeten The Deal

The Beginning

No one ever thinks divorce will happen to them. I never thought divorce would happen to me. I had a friend who was going through one at the same time I was. Her favorite thing to say, ad nauseum, was, "I didn't get married to get divorced." Huh. Really? 'Cause I did. I planned it from the start. I thought: If this doesn't work out, I'll just get a divorce. No big deal. You will find I have a sarcastic streak. Can't help it, get used to it. After about a thousand times of hearing this precious little phrase spouted from her lips, as though everyone else got married to get divorced, I wanted to knock this girl to kingdom come.

So there I was, 33 years old, three little kids, and divorced. My three boys were ages 2, 4, and 6 when I asked "the one who shall remain nameless" to leave. They were 3, 5 and 7 by the time the Big D was done. As all divorces are, mine was unfun. It was draining, depleting, and probably, as many would admit, too long in coming. I didn't even consider dating for about a year. I recognized that time and distance were the only things that would save others from my empty and exhausted self. So I took some time to regroup and redefine my new, single self.

And then came boredom. Now believe me, with three boys ages seven and younger, there was little time for true boredom. But there was this sense of boredom with being alone, or maybe it was just the evolution into readiness to date at all; of feeling whole and healed and happy with yourself. You find yourself with energy and restlessness that whisper in your ear, "It's time to get out there again."

And then you think, "Now what?" How do you even begin to date? I had begun accumulating single (divorced) friends. It is a real phenomenon how that happens. Once you have done the deed, single/divorced friends magically appear. It was either that or people started dropping like flies into divorce. I had a few single friends and we tried going out some. That is a weird and surreal experience. First of all, the bars you went to in your twenties are not the bars you want to go to now. You have to figure out where all of the age-appropriate men and women go and which nights are the "good nights."

Once we figured all this out, off we went. There were men who would ask for a phone number. If they "seemed normal" and I gave it out, most of the time there was never a call. There were the young men. At 33 and beyond, I began to feel like one of the oldest people in the bar or wherever. If a guy younger than 30 hit on me, I wanted to know what bet he was trying to win. It was a game, and it was not flattering or funny.

An aside: "Seems normal" became my new mantra. I start almost every weird, bad or scary date story with, "He seemed normal." It was a running joke almost immediately after I began dating.

Let me tell you a little bit about Pensacola, Florida. I grew up here and always thought it was a great place to live. I still think it is a great place to live. I have, however, a more defined perspective on dating in Pensacola. For those of you who are not aware of the Florida Panhandle, let me give you some examples of monikers linked to our area: The Emerald

Coast, The Whitest Beaches in the World, The Emerald City...good so far, right? Going on: Lower Alabama (sorry Alabama, but with your rap, it gives a different perspective), The Redneck Riviera, Home of Gay Pride...

Now the last three evoke some less-than-stellar images when it comes to dating, and specifically, dating for me. Let's just get the gay pride thing out of the way. I am all for gay pride. The only drawback for me is that we have a fairly high ratio of gay men in our area. This reduces my dating pool. Too bad really, because being a Democrat, I would have had a better chance of political alignment with a gay man than most straight men around here.

Speaking of political affiliation, I forgot to mention that we are also very red in the Florida Panhandle. We could even say blood red. I took a poll in my Sunday School class (which is remarkably evenly divided between Democrat and Republican) to see if dating outside your political affiliation is a deal breaker. My DEMOCRAT friend, Paige, voted an emphatic "Yes!" I am not totally sure, but it would be a challenge for me. The problem with this is that being in a RED area of the state, that would limit my dating pool to almost nil.

Okay, back to the Redneck Riviera. This little trait presents a problem for me because of the following dating standards without which I cannot live. The guy must:

1. Have an education. This means a degree, not high school, not an AA, and not trade school. This may sound harsh to some, but education is important to me, and I want my kids to have an example to follow.

2. Speak and write using correct grammar. This one has been a challenge. I am self-aware enough to know that I have an obsession with grammar. I do not expect perfection, but I have minimum standards. If a guy says "it don't" even once,

that's it. Around here, "it don't" is as common as a tan. I correct my sons' texts. I know it's obsessive but I have no desire to change it.

At any rate, I started doing online dating. It was scary and kind of fun all at once. At first I didn't tell anyone at all. I felt self-conscious. I thought maybe it meant I was desperate or unable to get my own date in the real world. But how does a single mother of three find the time to go out enough to meet anyone? I discovered that online dating made it easier to find people and get the initial contact out of the way. So it was my little secret.

After I created my profile (an agonizing process of writing who you are and what you want and finding a flattering photo), I immediately began getting message after message and wink after wink. A "wink" is like a message, but the guy or girl can send it without a message to let you know he/she is interested. I realized later that I was fresh meat. I had date after date. It is a good feeling to feel so popular and sought after, especially after the demoralizing experience of divorce. It made me feel young and attractive and fun. Things I hadn't felt in years.

After several years of starting and stopping the "online thing" as I like to call it, I had been joking that I was going to write about it. I decided to write this book so that these funny and bizarre experiences can be experienced by all. And you can learn from my hard-earned lessons and avoid some of the pitfalls of online dating. You really can't make this stuff up, and it is a story that needs to be told. I have accumulated nicknames for most of my stand-out dates. To give you a preview:

The Criminal Guy
The Sweeten the Deal Guy
BFD

Elizabeth Denham

The "Cheating" Guy
The Parking Lot Guy
The Fetish Guy: AKA Panty Hose Guy

Sweeten The Deal

The Sweeten the Deal Guy

Category 1: Too Much Too Fast.
Category 2: His Way or the Highway.
Category 3: Those Who Were Never Ready to Date.

Dating Tips:

1. *"Can you still have kids?" is not a first-date question.*
2. *Don't assume that a potential date has nothing better to do than wait on you to call to make last-minute plans. Even if that is true, the fact that you have given the indication that she is waiting with bated breath for your call is insulting or arrogant. Don't do it.*

I decided to start with the most outstanding date of all…he really wins the prize. This is one I could never, ever have made up. I think the title pretty much says it all. Sweeten the Deal Guy…think about it. Yes, he really said it.

This date was in the spring and, well, **he seemed normal**. He was an online date. He winked at me, so I checked out his profile. Marine Corps officer, pilot, law degree, same age as me, 5'7". Now, "he who shall remain nameless" was 5'7-1/2" standing tall. I am not opposed to less-than-tall men, but I enjoyed wearing heels again after eleven years with the same vertically challenged man.

This guy was a quick mover. Some online peeps like to email for weeks. Others go straight to the phone calls. Still others make a date without ever speaking. You just never know. This guy asked for my number right away and called within an hour. He asked me out for the same night. It was a little bit presumptuous to assume I had no other plans, but I went with it. He looked good on paper (words not to live by, by the way). I had a baseball game for one of the boys, but agreed to meet him after that since it was not my kid weekend.

He wanted to meet at the Wisteria. The Wisteria is a local watering hole on the road we, as kids, all knew as the "tree tunnel road." It sat tucked in the middle of an old neighborhood lined with huge oaks that covered the entire road in a canopy of limbs, and, in daylight, blocked out almost all of the sunlight. All of the locals knew it and had some story of youthful indiscretion there. I, however, being busy with three babies back-to-back-to-back, had never been to this bar. I knew it was a dive and *he* just happened to know that Papa John's delivered there. Classy, right? Actually, I was thinking it could be fun. We would have a low-key, pool-shooting, beer and pizza date. Could be fun and low pressure.

Oh, by the way, he went by the name "Big Frank."

So, I got to the Wisteria and Big Frank called on the way. He was right on time, always a good quality in a date. As he got out of his car, I could see that he looked exactly like his profile photo. Phew! Relief! This is not always the case. He got all the way out of the car, and huh. Big Frank was not so big. I am about 5' 6-1/2". Big Frank was at least a couple of inches shorter than me! So much for "big," right? Is this little white lie a deal breaker? I reserved judgment.

We went in and he ordered the pizza and beer. I looked around and it was about what I expected. Unfinished wood floors, well-worn tables, chairs with torn leather seats, and pool tables that may or may not be level. It was kind of dark and dank and you weren't quite sure your shoes would come up off the floor without sticking. You know--dive bar. There were customers who were "friends" with the bartender in a Norm, Cliff and Sam kind of way.

BIG RED FLAG

We sat to talk for a bit. He was nice enough, told me about his family, asked about mine. It is always a good sign when a date asks questions. I have learned that a total lack of interest in others as indicated by a lack of questions is a **BIG RED FLAG**. I was feeling slightly let down by the height fudge (but I kind of get why men would lie about that…just get me one foot in the door and I will win them over, right?), but generally optimistic. The one weirdly premature question was, *"Can you still have kids?"* What?

"Well, I can as far as I know," I said. Okay, this was taking a turn. He says, *"You are still capable?"*

"I haven't tried in a while, but I think so."

Okay, I have a few issues about that little dialogue. The bigger question should have been, "Do you want more kids?" I have three for goodness sake. And the ultimate question would be, "Would you want kids with me?" And this last one should be well into a relationship. These are not first-date questions, just in case others of you are lacking in common sense as it seems was Big Frank. My optimism began waning as I realized that this guy was on the fast track and may be more interested in a brood mare than a relationship.

So we ate pizza, shot pool and drank beer. The probing pregnancy questions abated and he was actually kind of funny. A decent date, a little off, but decent.

The next day, I had a horrible morning, a confrontation with "he who shall remain nameless" that left me depleted, hurt and embarrassed. It was at the ballpark (where you live when you have three boys) and it was so bad that an acquaintance asked me if I needed the police. I didn't, but I needed a distraction. I called my friend, Laura, and she invited me to her son's birthday party and offered me wine. The definition of a lifesaver, right? The party was outside at her house on the bay. The weather was perfect, not a cloud in the sky. Blue water and blue sky. I was not in charge of any children, and I got to sit in a lounge chair and breathe. After the party, she and I went for a quick drink to debrief before she met her boyfriend (who was one of my first online dates a couple of years before...too funny!) for dinner.

While we were having our wine at a little Gulf-side bar and watching the sun set (it was idyllic, really), Big Frank called. My very little, depleted bubble was about to burst. *Do you want to get together tonight?* This was probably 5:00. Hmm. Does he think I am sitting by the phone pining for his call? I really don't enjoy when guys assume you have no other plans and call at the last minute. Plan ahead, people!

I was tired and really not up for anything, but told him we could meet and have an early night. Laura said to invite him to dinner with them for a double date. I did, and he said, *"Well, what about after?"*

"After?"

"Yeah, after. What are we doing after?"

"Nothing. I am really tired."

"Well, if you want a second date, you are going to have to Sweeten the Deal," said Big Frank.

Long pause....and then....playing dumb because I got it right away, "What do you mean, 'Sweeten the Deal?' "

"Well, I fully expect to take you to dinner, buy you some drinks, and then after, go to your house and spend the night."

Another long pause....

"What are we, teenagers?" Big Frank kept going. *"Are we going to have an adult relationship or what?"*

Maybe it's just me, but I think that one reason teenage boys break up with teenage girls is because they won't put out...maybe I'm wrong.

Again, I say that I am really tired.

Big Frank added, *"Well, maybe you need to go home and go straight to bed."*

"I think I will," and I hung up.

Since that day, I have had several questions enter my mind as a better response than the ones I gave. I am one of those whose comebacks occur to the mind well after the time when they would be useful. One response: Where are you taking me and how much am I worth? Second response: Does this work for you often? Third response: Yes! I will have dinner with you (and then go spend as much of his money as possible and leave).

At the time, I wanted to cry when those words exited his mouth, but now, I love Big Frank. I mean, who could ever make this stuff up?

He is my favorite story ever.

But there are many more equally as strange...

Evolution

When I first started dating, and especially online dating, it was exciting. As I mentioned, you are fresh meat on the website. The minute the profile is done, it is like winning at the slot machine. Wink after wink and email after email.

In high school and college, I didn't date overly much. By my junior year of high school, I had a steady boyfriend, aka Stalker Guy, who lasted off and on for four years. That, however, is another story for another time. So, when I had a huge influx of date offers, I thought, hey, this is great! I didn't discriminate too much. If men asked me out and "**seemed normal**," I went.

Now I have learned a few things about men and the stages of evolution in dating. They fall into a few categories. There are those who are still very sad/mad/resentful about the last relationship ending. These men can't seem to stop talking about what really ticks them off about her. They spend way too much time talking, convincing, arguing about how they were wronged. They are victims of the highest order. Why they think this is a productive way to woo a woman is a mystery.

Then there are those who are in denial about some of their major issues. They are the king rationalizers who really don't want to face anything so that they can move on to a healthy relationship. They can lie about anything, from their actual relationship status to their education level to their height. It makes one wonder, where is the line in the sand? What is it okay to fudge (lie) about? Are you really having a business lunch with that woman or is it something else? And if someone would lie about something as obvious as his height (Big Frank), then why not lie about the girlfriend he sees on his off days?

Next would be those who just want to get married. They jump in immediately, too much too fast, and you get the feeling that they don't really care who they are with as long as it is someone. These guys can be put on speakerphone and never know you went to take a shower. That, I tell you, really makes a girl feel special, especially when he ends up married within the year after you tell him to take a hike. Point made?

So as the years went by, I learned how to spot these slippery suckers. I didn't really do as much small talk. I got more to the point, and if a guy said something odd, I asked about it.

For example, there is a question on the profile about how much you drink: never, socially, moderately, daily. "Daily" is a **BIG RED FLAG**. I don't even have to explain that. But "never" is also a **BIG RED FLAG.** "Never" usually means someone has had a problem. In the beginning, if there was a "never," I would ask about it.

"So, do you have a problem with alcohol?"

If it was a "yes," I got through the date, and that was that. I forgot to mention that one of my criteria was no addictive behaviors or any behavior that required "-aholic" as a descriptive ending. Besides, I really wanted to have a glass of wine with dinner sometimes, and I wanted a guy who could have one with me...or at least pour it for me! After a while, I didn't even respond to anyone who marked "never." Statistically, it was a loss.

Another important question was "How long have you been divorced or separated?" This is important because the recently divorced always think they are ready for something new, and THEY ARE NOT! And you can't convince them that they are not. Okay, I know, some people move into a new relationship quickly, but that is the exception, not the rule. I have years of dating experience to back this up, so just take my word for it.

To be clear, I did not think these generalizations encompassed all men. I knew there were good ones out there, or I would have ceased to persist. However, I am just saying people have issues. You just have to attempt to find the one with the least offensive ones or at least the ones most compatible with your own.

The Criminal

Category 1: The Great Omission.

Category 2: Those who are too busy telling you how great they are to notice how great you are.

Category 3: Those who should just keep their own company.

Dating Tips:

1. *Meet unknown dates in a public place.*
2. *Know the guy's first and last name.*
3. *Tell at least one friend where you are and who you are with.*
4. *No guy wants to "watch a movie at my house."*

This is the guy that you know must be out there, but you really don't believe he will happen to you. This guy is the reason you meet blind dates in a public place and have your friends prepared to call you with an "emergency." The problem is, he flies under the radar until after the first (or second or third) date, so that you really don't know he has a dark side unless you luck into this shady information. He is not the norm, but he is definitely out there and you must be vigilant…or lucky…

The Criminal was one of my early dates in the foray back to singledom. He **seemed normal.** He was my age, from Pensacola (like me), educated and a business and home owner. Interestingly, he was also running for City Council. This appealed to me because I thought it showed a sense of social responsibility and a desire to get involved in the community. Yea him!

He emailed only a few times online and made a quick date. I told my sisters all about my big date as usual. My sisters generally got the inside scoop about my dating life such as it was. Maybe I should have felt sorry for them...hmmm, I'll think about that later.

So my date and I met at Bonefish Grill. Good place for a date, I thought, close to my house, well populated, a cross between a restaurant and a bar. Good lighting. Soft, you-can-talk-above-it background music. The date was fine. He looked close enough to his picture. I am pretty sure he was a good bit younger in the pic...still, close enough. We had good conversation, he told me all about his time living in Atlanta and working as a cop. He loved living in a bigger city and was really devoted to his work. He told me all about his political campaign. He was excited to be running and was the "youngest candidate in the race!" He told me about his family, his college and his departure to Atlanta and return to Pensacola. He was really great! I didn't get to talk much, but oh well.

After we had a drink or two, he said, *"You want to go watch a movie at my house?"*

It was a bit abrupt, and I realize now what a line this was and how many men actually use it. Believe me, I learned to be a lot more aware and suspicious after this particular date.

Anyway, idiot that I was, I said, "Sure." So, we went by the convenience store to grab beer.

LITTLE RED FLAG THAT BECAME A BIG RED FLAG

He sent me in to the convenience store with money (at least I didn't have to pay) because the lady behind the counter just couldn't stand him. He had no idea why. This, I thought, was odd. Very odd.

BIG RED FLAG

We got to his house and he told me his grandmother had left it to him. It was in a little cul-de-sac off one of the roads that cut through town from one mall to the other. It was a nice, brick, ranch-style house in a decent neighborhood. We walked in through a bare garage into the kitchen. He had campaign signs, flyers and postcards strewn all over the counter and kitchen table. We got a beer, put the others in the fridge and went to the living room. It was a typical guy's pad--extra-large TV, too many videos on the shelf and not many decorations. He did have fluffy, flowery couches he had inherited from his grandmother along with a hodgepodge of other old lady touches...cut-glass lamps, cross-stitched throw pillows. He turned on the TV (he didn't turn on any lights) and of course, within five minutes of sitting on the couch, he tried to make a move. Ugh, but okay, lesson learned about the man-code about movie-watching. The I'm-an-idiot feeling washed over me as I was politely trying to redirect his attention to the movie, when just in the nick of time my phone rang! It was my sister. I didn't answer, and she called back immediately...three times. This actually gave me a good excuse to answer without seeming rude. There must be something going on, right? Who calls that much that quickly? She actually does, but he didn't know that.

"Hello?"

"You need to get in the car right now and call me when you do."

"What?"

"You need to get in the car right now and call me when you do."

"What? What are you talking about?"

"Just do it!"

Well, this was weird. What do I do? What could she possibly have to tell me? But, what do you do in this situation? In a split second, I decided that you flee your date in the least rude way possible and trust your sister. So, I made an excuse about it being a work night and getting the kids off to school the next day. It was 10 or 10:30 at night, so it seemed reasonable, I think.

When I called Kathryn on my way home, I got an earful. In her infinite desire to do research and her curiosity about this guy's political platform (she seriously loves politics and is seriously good at research), she had Googled my date. Apparently Mr. City Council wannabe had been arrested in Atlanta where he worked as a jailer, not a cop. There is a difference. A big one.

BIG FAT LIE

He had been arrested for shooting two boys through the plate glass of a convenience store. He thought they were armed, but it was a toy gun. He was convicted on a lesser count than the original charge, but convicted nonetheless. This was very unsettling news. In an effort to be fair, I thought about the stories you read in the news, and I know that things are not always what they seem and that plea deals are made to avoid the risk of more severe punishment. I needed more information before casting any judgment. I will admit, it would have been difficult for me to have another date with him even before I discovered more. But I was trying to give the benefit of the doubt.

THE TRUTH

I had a friend in the police department who ran a background check the next day. The guy also had arrests for beating three former girlfriends; the most recent, a live-in girlfriend six months before our date. He was attending anger management classes and was not allowed in any establishment that served alcohol.

So it was all clear now...the reason for the quick date at Bonefish...he was taking a big risk drinking out in public, yet he was trying to **seem normal.** Sending me into the convenience store for beer eliminated any risk for him; and the desire to drink said beer at his house, out of the public eye, was completely safe.

TRUE COLORS

The next evening, he called. I felt a little sick to my stomach because I was never so lucky to have something just disappear. I had to deal with it, but I wasn't prepared. I didn't answer the phone, needing time to decide how to handle this wacko situation. He left a nice message asking me to call back when I could. Ten minutes later he called again. This message was an attempt to leave the same normal message as before, but I could hear the irritation in his voice. Ten minutes after that, he was ticked that I didn't answer. He left a message demanding to know where I was and why I was not answering his messages. Now as far as he knew, we had a decent date the day before and I could have been busy doing anything.

MY BIG FAT LIE

As much as I did not want to deal with The Criminal, and as scary as his escalating messages were, I knew I had to respond in some way. I knew that he would probably continue to escalate. I decided to avoid speaking to him altogether since he was already volatile. I sent him an email telling him that I had been seeing someone else casually, and we decided to make it exclusive. That way, it was not about him, and I was off the hook.

Justified? I think so! And it worked. No more calls.

My poor sister took a lot of flak for her little online investigation. My dad was especially vocal in telling her to just let it go. He was sure it wasn't that big of a thing and she should let me figure out my own dates. I think the word "busybody" may have even been used.

After all of this, we said to my sister....Google, Kathryn, Google!

Safety, Safety, Safety

I figured the chapter after The Criminal would be a good time to discuss general rules of safety for online dating. While I do not believe that every potential date is a Ted Bundy, I do believe a little common sense goes a long way. And if you set some hard and fast rules for yourself, it lets you off the hook when guys ask you to do things with which you are not quite comfortable. You can just blame the rules. Takes the pressure off. So here they are:

1. **Always know your date's first name, last name and cell phone number.** If he is unwilling to give you this information in the interest of your safety, then he must have something to hide. A true gentleman will offer it so that you feel comfortable.

2. **Always tell a friend your plans.** Before every date, I would call my friend Tara and report my time, location, date's name and date's phone number. She did the same for her dates. Someone needs to know where you are just in case. Often I would even joke to my date that I had this little ritual. Never hurts to let them know someone is watching.

3.   Do not let a guy pick you up from your house on the first date...or second date...or maybe even third date. This is pretty obvious, but do you want a guy like "The Criminal" knowing where you live? I know it's not that hard to find out where people live these days, but at least make them work for it.

4.   Do not ride in a car with a guy on a first date. Having your own car is just smart. Consider it the getaway car--not just in case of danger, but also in the case of total weirdness. Read on to see what I mean. And pay close attention to BFD.

5.   Do not ride on a boat, or go to a beach or lake or river on a first date. Too easy to hide the body. I am joking. Well, kind of.

6.   Always meet your date in a public place. Refer back to number 4. Not so easy to hide the body.

7.   Always meet your date in a place with which you are familiar. You might run into people you know, and while you may feel like you have an audience, he will think you know everyone in town. And witnesses are always good. Plus, you know all of the exits.

These rules are not designed to scare you away from online dating. I think online dating is fun and entertaining with the right attitude (I will discuss the "right" attitude later). But knowing how to keep yourself safe is paramount in any situation. And as I said, a little common sense goes a long way.

You will know when it is time to loosen the grip.

The Married Guy

Category 1: Liar liar pants on fire.

Category 2: Those who are not ready to date (obvious, right?).

Category 3: Those who fail to embrace their own reality.

Dating Tips:

1. *Follow your own rules.*
2. *You should have a rule that you do not speak to someone who doesn't have a profile picture.*
3. *Do not email with a potential date for too long (no more than a week).*

That pretty much says it all, doesn't it? For once, I did not start the story with, "Well, he seemed normal." This experience was brief and a little nauseating for me. He was on a dating site. He wrote a message, but had no picture posted. I had a firm policy that if you had no picture posted, I didn't respond. This policy was a necessary one because I had become cynical (but not too cynical) enough (but apparently not cynical ENOUGH – it's confusing, I know) to want to know with whom I am speaking. When you have enough bad dates, you start to wonder if it is someone you have been out with before or someone you know.

In this case, I broke the rule [Big Mistake]. I wrote back because his profile seemed interesting. He was interested in the arts – music and ballet. Hey, I liked those things. He was educated. We all know how important that was to me. He could put together a good sentence. Among the many profiles containing atrocious grammar, this was refreshing. So I wrote back and asked for a picture. In the process, I gave him my email address because he didn't know how to attach a photo to the dating-site email [**Big Red Flag #1**] and he didn't want to post one to his profile [**Big Red Flag #2**].

When I received his pictures, I began to see why he hadn't posted any. He was a little shorter, a lot older and a little more frog-like than I had hoped (he had no neck and this, in turn, made him appear Kermit-ish). I was fairly certain he lied about his age and a posted photo would have outed this little indiscretion. And to me, any lie is too big of a lie, especially in the getting-to-know-you phase of dating.

I had already decided to get off of the dating site for a while. I had discovered that I only had a limited store of the energy required to communicate with strangers, get geared up for a date, find a sitter and actually go on the date before I needed to take a break! So after a very few emails, I took my profile down and that was the end of that.

Or not.

Soon after my last email with Married Guy, I received an email from someone I didn't know, and it was signed with both the husband's and wife's names. It took a moment to wade through the confusion, because, really, who expects this to happen? Therein lies the part of me that was still not cynical ENOUGH. Or maybe you could have called me gullible, who knows? I liked to think I had just not lost my ability to see the good in people. I knew after a moment exactly who it was from and why it was sent. Sickness in the pit of my stomach set in and not out of guilt. How would I know he was Married Guy, after all? It was more to do with the fact that married men do this kind of thing. I know that they do, as my experience with marriage was not replete with faithfulness, but still, I don't expect this behavior...gullible?

At any rate, I found the undeleted emails in my inbox...how lucky that I never deleted! So I am going to print them verbatim because, really, you can't make this stuff up!

The First Email from "The Couple"

Hello, I hope that I have the correct e-mail address. Your name, e-mail address was given to my husband as a piano instructor. I was wondering if you teach piano lessons in the Panama City, Fl area? If so, do you have any openings for our daughter who is 10 yrs old. She began with her first piano lessons last year with [name deleted to protect the innocent]. *However, she, presently has no openings. My daughter shows great interest in learning to play the piano and would love to continue to take lessons. Please let me know if you are a piano teacher (I hope that I have the right e-mail address) and if so, if you have any availability for my daughter & myself to meet with you for her to possibly take piano lessons from you.*

Thank you so much and we look forward to hearing from you.

[Signed Wife and Husband]

[Now how do you respond to this? I knew exactly what had happened, but I really didn't want to be involved. She is

31

very cagey in this email because she makes it clear that she is married to him, that he has lied and she knows it, that they have a daughter and that she expects a response. This is a suspicious woman!]

My Response

Hi there,

I am sorry. I don't teach piano. I don't even play piano. Good luck in your search.

[Maybe that will be the end, right? Wrong. And I knew it.]

Response from The Wife

Thank you so much Elizabeth for answering my email so quickly. I was wondering if you know my husband [name changed to protect the guilty]? I found a piece of paper with your email address on it with another name [name changed to protect the innocent…or is she guilty, who knows?] . *He told me that someone had given it to him because he was trying to find a piano teacher for our daughter. I didn't believe him & that's his own fault! I'm so sorry to bother you if I have done so. As you can see I don't trust my husband, rightfully so because he has cheated on me in the past with a 24 yr old woman who was in Annex Jail & a druggie! Do you know my husband? He is nearly 54 yrs old, light blonde/brown hair nearly bald, blue eyes & wears glasses. He is retired, works out @ Gold's Gym on 23rd St in Panama City, Fl. He plays Bluegrass Music, guitar, banjo & cello.*

We have a home for sale in Lynn Haven, Fl. If you would like I can send you a photo of him. Please let me know how you know him. As I don't Trust him with legitimate reasons! I sincerely Thank you for your time, & help in my uncomfortable situation. I am Truly Sorry to bother you.

Sincerely, [the wife]

[At this point, her sentence structure and random use of capital letters was getting on my nerves. And really? You have to ask if you are bothering me? No, really, this is so much fun. And what's with all of the random details? Why did I need to know that he works out at Gold's Gym and that their home in Lynn Haven was for sale? And I seriously didn't need to know that the last mistress was literal jail bait. Before I could think of how to respond to this one, she sent a picture of the two of them for confirmation that it was, in fact, him. It was him alright! He was standing tall (well, as tall as he could stretch). And she was towering over him, wearing the tiniest little spaghetti-strapped top with the biggest fake boobs that I had ever seen overflowing it.]

My Response

Hi [the wife],

I am very sorry to read your last email. I also saw the picture. I was on an online dating site. Your husband wrote to me and sent a photo. We wrote a couple of times, but I decided to stop online dating, and didn't write him back after that. I never spoke to him on the phone and never met him. I do not live in Panama City. He had wanted to meet for dinner or to play tennis.

I am sorry you are going through this. I am a single mother, just trying to date a little. It is disappointing to know that there are married men on these sites.

[At this point I just hoped it ended here, but no, she was a persistent little sucker.]

Wife's Response

Dear Elizabeth, Do you know if he is still on that website? If so, I have a plan on how I'm going to catch him & put an end to all of his Deceit! Please let me know when you Last received an email from him. Please if you can, forward me a copy of the photo that he sent to you. I Promise you that he will Never Know that you ever sent it to me! Thank you so much Elizabeth. Sincerely, [the wife]

[I sent her the pictures he sent me.]

Wife's Response

The pretty little girl next to him with the tux on is my Daughter on Our Wedding Day! The cute little girl in the boat is My Daughter, not his biological child. His daughter nearly 15 yrs old is in the 3rd photo down in a booth next to him! The New Escalade that he is leaning against is my car. The skirt that he is holding up is from when we were @ a Bluegrass Festival in LiveOak, Fl, in March/April 09.

He is Not 45 yrs old like he has listed! He is 10 Yrs Older! Nearly 54 Yrs Old! He hasn't been Self Employed since 2000!

He's retired & is trying to get his Insurance License back & needs to find I job! What a Deceitful Man I'm Married to! Thank you so much Elizabeth for your Kindness & Honesty towards me...When did you Last have Contact with Him, my husband? It is So Important!

That was enough. I wrote her and told her I was at work and really needed to get back to it. She wrote one more time to tell me that she had found his profile on the dating site and had hatched a plan to catch him. A plan? Really? I can only imagine what happened. Once she began to discuss the idea of a "plan to catch him," I lost a little respect. She had already caught him. She had enough information, but she fell into the trap of the drama. She had sunk to his level. She had to get him back. It was mortifying to have the entire conversation, but I really did feel sorry for her (well, almost). She had already been through his betrayal, and instead of being strong enough to just leave or even to confront him, she put herself through this convoluted game of cat and mouse.

Side Note – Another Married Guy...maybe!

Sometimes you don't even get to the date before you realize something is not "normal." I had a guy who wrote to me, made plans and talked about how excited he was to meet me. He was going to call during a break at work, and after work we were going to dinner and a movie. I never got a call during the break, and he never called after work. I decided to email and just see if something had come up, and his entire profile was deleted from the dating site. So, I am thinking he was found out by a wife or girlfriend...what do you think? Heehee!

Why My Dad Makes Dating Harder

My dad is a big man...and I don't mean big physically. I mean he is a man with a presence. He walks into a room and not only do people pay attention, they listen. I don't think I always realized this effect he has on people.

Growing up, he was the dad who danced down the hallway in his boxers. He was the dad who came to the ball games and the ballet recitals. He used to let all five of us kids take turns having Saturday morning breakfast with him at his office and playing at his secretary's desk while he worked. When I was in high school, we had a dinner/dance at church, and he was about fourth in a Conga line of guys from my youth group dancing to "The Grapevine" from the California Raisin commercial. I remember all of those things vividly. He was the fun, funny dad that showed up.

One of the favorite family stories is when he had strung an electric fence around the horse field. He is not mechanically inclined and just didn't believe it was going to work. He hopped on his horse, rode to the end of the field and proceeded to touch the wire. Well, it worked, and we looked up to see him marching back to the barn carrying one rein and seeing red, furious that he was thrown from the horse. Common sense is not his strong suit.

These are the fun and silly memories of a young girl.

What I have learned as I have gotten older is that he is a great man. As I look back on experiences in my life, things that seemed mundane at the time are more significant in seeing who he is as a whole. I appreciated the time he went to Tate High School to talk to the dean who didn't think a girl should take calculus because she didn't need it to graduate. He fixed it, of course, in his diplomatic and kind way so that the dean didn't even realize he had been confronted.

I watched him stand up for each of us to teachers, parents, church leaders...anyone who had not treated us fairly or kindly. I remember talks with my sisters' soccer coach, my geometry teacher, and my brother's various teachers. He stood up for my brother to a leader of the church who had made some very bad decisions.

These are things a young girl thinks a dad just does.

As you mature and live more life, you realize that these are not things that all dads do.

My dad worked a lot of hours in his law practice. He built a strong and successful practice. As I worked for him off and on throughout my life, I understood the demands of his job. I began to realize the effort it took for him to be at everything we did, to meet every need and to be there when we needed him to stand up for us. Five of us.

He also insisted that each of us do the right thing. When my brother and his friend prank- called a cop (really, who has that kind of luck?) he made them go to his house and apologize. He and my mother were there for every bad decision or mistake that we all made. He tried to teach us all to do the things every parent wants their children to do: be honest, be honorable, follow through, stand up for those who can't stand for themselves, keep your promises.

What I didn't realize as a child was that he was teaching us these things by doing them. I began to see him more as a whole person after working with him. He does not do business with those who lie, cheat or steal. He would never take advantage of someone less fortunate than himself. If there is even a question of character or honor in a decision, he will take the high road even when it is to his own detriment. I have seen him sacrifice time and money to avoid even the mere hint of impropriety.

In being an honorable man, he has built a life filled with people who respect him.

He lived in town and wore a suit to work every day. He lived in the country and wore work-boots and flannel shirts. He treated each group of people with equal amounts of respect and kindness. Each group, when seeing him in the other locale, was surprised at his appearance. I have never seen him think he is superior.

By living life as he knows he should, he has earned accolades in his career. He has been at Senate hearings to speak about people infected with HIV by blood companies. He has sat on national steering committees. He has earned many legal awards. He has had a local legal award named after him.

The awards and accolades themselves are not what is important or impressive (though they are), but what is impressive is that honor still matters. In trying to date in today's world of excess and entitlement and doing whatever it takes to get ahead, it shows that the nice guy still wins. Doing the right thing still matters.

He is completely devoted to my mother. They have been married almost 45 years. The idea of them not devoted to each other is not even in the realm of possibility. I grew up secure in that--never a doubt. I hope that someday my kids know that kind of stability.

The bad part about having a dad like mine is that the bar is set incredibly high. I eventually learned that the man I married did not have any of the honor that I thought he did. In dating, I have had tons of funny and, well, tragically bad and hilarious dates. I will write about them all. The ones I don't write about are the ones that aren't particularly bad, but the men just don't measure up. They have not accomplished anything. I am not necessarily talking about financial success. I am talking about success as a person. They are rude to people. They blur the lines of truth thinking that the little lies don't matter. I think they do.

I don't think that there are many men like my dad. I think people in general have gotten lazy and take the easy way. Doing the right thing is usually not the easiest thing. Doing the right thing when no one is looking is even harder. But that is the definition of character...doing the right thing when no one is looking. My dad does that.

And that set my standard.

Cry Baby, Cry

Category 1: This one has me stumped, but I think it is "People who think they are sensitive, but really they are just dumbasses."

Category 2: Those who are too insecure to date.

Dating Tips:

1. *Don't have a dramatic build-up to a non-dramatic story. It sets up immediate disappointment. And you look like a drama queen.*
2. *Lunch-hour dates are a good idea.*
3. *Be aware of poor-pitiful-me syndrome. AKA beware of the victim. Trying to be with someone who is hell-bent on feeling sorry for himself is a no-win situation.*

So, he **seemed normal**. He wrote to me online with a very general introduction: *Hi, I like your profile, I would really like to talk to you.* The usual. He asked for my number fairly quickly and started texting.

And he texted a lot.

BIG RED FLAG

I think it is better to start to talk or text sooner than later. Some men get stuck in email communication forever and nothing ever moves along. I have theories about this that I will address later. I just don't see the point. I don't need fifteen pen pals. I just want one good date! Asking a lot, I know. But there is also the too-much-too-fast syndrome.

So Cry Baby texted. And he texted. And he texted. I would get, *"Good Morning!"* first thing every morning. And then:

How are you?
Are you busy at work?
Sorry for the long pause, I had a busy spell.
Are you busy?
Have a nice lunch!
How was lunch?
Busy this afternoon?
Are you off work yet?

Now, I guess he was thinking this was fun and he was attentive. I was thinking, okay, thanks for the interest but sheesh, I have work to do. Don't get me wrong. I liked to text and talk and have someone attentive. I think it just bothered me when it was inane conversation. During the work day. When I was trying to work. Or maybe it was because it felt attention seeking. Or maybe the expectation of my response within certain acceptable time periods (designated by him) made him seem needy. Or maybe it was just because he was the wrong person. Yep, I think that's it, wrong person.

So lunch at the Ale House. Ale House is a family-style restaurant during the day with long wooden booths, pool tables and outdoor decks. There are TVs scattered throughout, so it's a fun game-day hang out. At night, it turns more toward a bar, but for lunch, good first date place, I think. Casual, quick and easy. It started off fine. He looked like his photo. Good! He was polite. Yea! Sat down and ordered a bucket of beer. Woohoo! Off to a decent start.

Don't get too excited, though, because after all, he made the blog, and well, you saw the title.

The date started off with the usual small talk. Where are you from? What do you do? He told me about his job in the military working with electronics. He emphasized that he worked with his hands. This becomes important in the blink of an eye.

Because in the blink of an eye, the tide turned.

"Your nails are very beautiful," he said.

Weird, but okay. Never had a guy compliment my nails. Maybe he's gay and doesn't know it, but wait! He is a Republican. That can't be it. And see? I was trying not to lock myself in by my politics and be open-minded.

"Speaking of that (the nails), *I have something to tell you,"* he said.

Oh crap! It is a segue.

"I have an injury."

BIG RED FLAG

The mind reeled. The possibilities for the coming explanation are limitless and all rolled through my mind at remarkable speed. Head injury? Boy parts injury? This is what the military job conjures up. Nothing was visible to my eye...and it was preceded by the "speaking of the nails" comment. I was mystified.

"This is really hard for me to tell you. It is difficult for me to talk about," he added. *"But I feel like it is something I should tell you."*

Okay. Let's stop right there for a minute. In general, I think there is very little that warrants this kind of dramatic interjection on a first date. Much less five minutes into a first date. After all, the purpose of a first date is to determine whether you want a second date. If that determination is "no," then why reveal your deepest, darkest secrets? It's unnecessary and well, embarrassing. And do you really need another soul walking on this Earth with your deepest, darkest secrets? The answer is "no."

Moving on.

He went on to explain that he was on a pontoon boat a few months ago and got his finger caught in something on the boat. Part of the finger was ripped off. Evidently, this is not an uncommon occurrence on pontoon boats. When I asked which one, he quickly flashed his pinky finger at me and hid it away. I would never have noticed a thing if he hadn't pointed it out. He was barely missing anything. The last knuckle may have been gone (or less), but the finger was still pretty normal looking.

Maybe now I should say, the finger **seemed normal**...

He went on with the following:

"It really set me back for a while, but then I decided I would overcome. I can still throw a ball. I can still grip a cup. I was depressed for a while, but I'm better now."

For some reason, I had shifted my eyes down to the table. I am in favor of eye contact during a conversation, but there are times when it is better to avert your eyes and conceal your reaction rather than risk the uncontrolled eye-roll or look of confusion. "Keep your expression expressionless," I commanded myself. I have a tendency to broadcast whatever is going through my mind on my face. It is not a good trait. Or maybe it is. It makes me a terrible liar. After his little explanation of the injury, he started to say something else, but was rendered unable to speak. I looked back up and realized he was choked up. He began wiping the tears from his eyes with his napkin. Tried to speak again, wiped more tears instead.

Seriously? I have heard of men crying in their beer, but good grief...it should at least be over a football game! How is one supposed to react to this little episode? All I could think was, "Get a bigger problem, dude!"

So I launched into this little, "It's okay, we all have our crosses to bear" speech. "It's fine, not a big deal." Really. REALLY. NOT A BIG DEAL.

I am sure that his accident hurt and that it was very traumatic at the time, but are you kidding me? Crying on a first date? Ugh! And why the urgent need to tell me this information? This screamed, too much too fast!

I continued to "relate" using my youngest son's seizure disorder as an example of a man (he is seven, by the way) having to overcome an obstacle. I told a brief version of his diagnosis (seizing on the hour every hour for two weeks) and our success in getting it controlled (thank God) and how brave he was when he had to deal with testing and needles and EEGs. I described how he lives a normal life even in the face of adversity. Hint, hint.

Sadly, my little Cry Baby didn't understand what I was trying to say to him...a pinky finger is NOT A BIG DEAL!!!!!

After we ate and I was pulling out of the parking lot to turn left, he pulled out turning right. I was on the phone. I smiled and waved. Never thought about it again.

About five hours later Cry Baby called.

"I saw when you were in the car on the phone that you had a big laugh," he said.

BIG, ENORMOUS, GLARING RED FLAG

"Yes."

"Well, I was wondering what you were laughing at."

Are you kidding? I was actually proud of him for waiting so many hours. It must have been killing him.

I had called my mother back and was talking about my other son. My son was in a Broadway-style chorus and had to sing and dance. At 10 years old, he independently decided that ballet would help his performance with the chorus. In the process of taking classes, he had decided to audition for the Nutcracker. My mother and I were discussing the audition and laughing because he was so funny and dedicated. She didn't even know I was on the date.

The reason I even mention what I was actually talking about on the phone call is this: a first date is not something that drives your whole existence. It does not even drive your day. Or even the five minutes after your first date. I will discuss this more later, but the fact is, that first date did not change the priority of my sons in my day. I went back to the things that I do on a regular basis--check in on my parents, my kids and my friends. Good or bad, it was just a date.

So back to the call.

"Okay," he said. *"I just thought maybe you were nice to my face, and then you were laughing behind my back."*

45

My head hurts.

I was not the most secure person when it came to men and dating, but I knew waaaaay better than to ever say something like that. One date. Two hours. Lunch. You don't get to ask me what I was talking about on the phone in the car. Sorry. It's a rule.

The next day he texted. First one was during church. Second one was during a parent meeting. Third one was while I was at a movie with a friend. The third one said, *"Did I do something wrong? Are you ignoring me?"*

After the third one, I answered.

"No, not ignoring you, just busy. And I wanted to say thank you so much for the nice date, but I don't think we are a good fit. Good luck."

His response? *"Why do you say that? Be honest."*

Does he really want to know? Don't think so, as indicated by this next text:

"I deleted my online profile last night. I don't like it. It just doesn't feel right."

"I deleted my profile" is not a comment that follows "Why do you say that." It goes from wanting to know what went wrong to wanting to be a victim. Not just a cry baby, but a whiner, too.

I did not respond.

I did not write this story right away. It took a little more than a month to get around to it. About a week after I wrote it and published it on my blog, I checked the comments section. I vaguely remembered that sometime during the tearful lunch, I had mentioned that I wrote about my bad dates. Apparently what little self-awareness the crier had was in knowing that I would probably write about a grown man who cried on a first date. I found the following (verbatim):

The beauty of the story, is that there are always two sides. One side can be just as you described above. But the other, takes a whole different stance. First, I will admit up front that this person is me. I am in no way ashamed of anything I did or said. Just as I defend your right to free speech, I would like to exercise my right to free speech as well. I hardly doubt that you have the guts to leave this up for people to read.

First, let me say that I was leary of meeting people from online anyway. My theory is that is they are good people, their friends or coworkers or people they associate with will always be looking for good people to hook them up with. So that is the reason for the texting and phone calls. I wanted to truly get to know someone before I met them in person. I wasn't truly ready to meet anyone, but I was pressured and gave in. My fault.

Second, I am still a little taken aback by what happened to me. I am still in a lot of pain on a daily basis and it's not healing on the inside correctly. I am in pain everyday. Not to most people, maybe it's not a big deal, but to me, a guy that works with his hands and played some type of sport a minimum of 5 days a week, it is VERY traumatic to me. To quote from Michelle Obama, 'Everyone grieves at their own pace." (oh my, did a Republican just use a quote from a Democrat, and he knew to put the period inside the quotation mark? How did he know to do that?) I digress. The bottom line is that we should never criticize people until we walk a minute in their own shoes. I can only hope that you are not raising your children with these same judgments. Oh and another note, due to my military status, there is a potential that I will lose my job and not be allowed to reenlist. So there is added pressure from that, but I plan to fight as much as I can because I am not a quitter. Women say they want a nice guy, but then they meet one that is truly nice and sensitive, then use that against him to pick on him and make fun of him. Not nice!

[And then…a second comment]

Now on to the comment about me asking you what you were laughing about. This is a situation that was a calculated move. The very minute I found out about your blog, I knew exactly what you were up to. You are using POF, not to actually meet a nice guy, but to get guys to take you out so you can nit pick their actions and mannerisms solely for the purposes of writing your blog. GIGANTIC RED FLAG!! Anyway, I knew what was going on and I wanted to see if you had the guts to admit to my face what you were saying. I knew you wouldn't.

Same thing goes for the texts the next day, I knew that I wouldn't ever see you again, because I wasn't interested anyway. There are many red flags your way that I hesitate to mention, only because that is not what this email is about. It isn't about what you bring to the table as a potential mate, it is about what you are doing on a daily basis to put others down solely to make yourself feel better. Perhaps, you have been scorned by a man and this is your way to get even, feel free. You call yourself a Christian and go to church, yet among all this, have you ever asked what God would think about this? Jesus walked with the poor, the handicapped, the lame, and the wicked so he could be a positive influence on them and teach them the ways of the Lord. What are you doing?

[And another comment]

About me saying I am deleting my POF (which I did do) it wasn't to wine in any way at all. It was because my theory was correct and I wanted to avoid temptation from meeting more people who deep down, don't really have it together.

You have so eloquently described me above, now allow me the chance to tell you what I truly am. A nice guy, with character and morals, non-judgmental (even to democrats! JK) Funny, a hard worker with a good job and good credit, a homeowner, with minimal debt, down to earth and fun loving, college educated, patriotic and all around good guy with a good heart. I have worked very hard to get where I am and I am very secure in my position in life. I will never let anyone bring me down. I am the person that brings people around me up, not vice versa. I will pray that the pain in your heart be healed soon, but "We all grieve at our own pace!"

Please pardon me for any errors, I am not an English major nor did I proof read it. I only wrote what was in my heart.

He wrote these comments using his real name. Why, oh why?

My Comment in Response:

(Name changed to protect Cry Baby), I am very sorry that you read this and that your feelings were hurt. I have never used a real name and never would. I would like to clarify a couple of things. First, I am not dating to write a blog. Many of the dates about which I have written happened years ago. In dealing with dating, I have had so many awful experiences that I have learned to use levity. I would love a great date. I would love to find someone to whom I can relate. I try to be optimistic about every experience, but if you read the other entries, I have had dates with married people, criminals and perverts.

Second, I am not sure who pressured you to meet, but it wasn't me. You asked and I agreed.

Third, I am very sorry that you are so traumatized by your finger. I do think that perspective is a great thing. I see my disability clients daily who are in so much pain that they can't walk or sit, much less work. I have family members who experience debilitating pain daily. I have watched and worried about the health of a child for the last five years. I cannot relate to your belief that the loss of the tip of a finger is that traumatic. I will take responsibility for my difficulty with that.

Last, I was not laughing at you on my phone call. I was, as I said, talking about my son. It didn't occur to me to get on the phone and talk about you.

This blog has been written to bring some lightness and humor to the unpleasant world of dating. I am very sorry that you were hurt.

I don't think there is much to say except that being caught on a bad date blog by one of your subjects is less than ideal. I do think that his comments perfectly illustrated his victim mentality. For example, how can a grown man be "pressured" into online dating? To make what happens not his fault. Enough said.

Some people (Cry Baby) seem to think that the fact that I wrote these stories down is mean. The thing is, life is funny. Dating is funny. Online dating is even funnier. I did my best to make sure that the men I dated were not identified by the things I wrote. So many people have had less than stellar dates. So many people have told me that they have a story I should include. And I think that if you can't laugh at life then you begin to take it too seriously.

And that is just bad…

Scare Tactic or Screening Tool

Many people who knew about my blog thought I should have used a pen name. Most of them also thought I should never have told anyone (especially single men) about it. I had mixed feelings about these suggestions.

As for the pen name, I pretty much decided that if I had to endure dates like these, I should get credit for it. After all, I don't know any one of my single girlfriends who has been asked to "put out" in order to get a second date. I don't think anyone has ever cried on a first date with any of my friends. This is not to say that my friends don't have their own uniquely horrifying bad date stories, but these are my stories, and I am, after all , the one telling them! Now that I think about it, the bigger question may be what kind of magnetic draw I had that attracted such unique men...but that's another question for another day.

As for men being afraid of being outed on my blog, I was not being rude to any of these dates. And I never told one of them off, as tempting as it was...not even Sweeten the Deal Guy. I did try to get out of the situations as graciously and as painlessly as possible. I have not used real names, nor have I given identifying information, so I think I'm good.

My sister thought I should never, ever tell a guy, especially a date, about the blog. She thought I would never have another date and if I did, he would run scared if told my little secret. I really had to mull over what I thought about telling single guys about my blog. Was this a subconscious form of self-sabotage? Or did I really believe that a normal, secure guy would get as big a kick out of these stories as I did? I kept coming back to one thought: Any guy intimidated by the blog must relate to one or more of the stories. If there was even a hint of fear that he would show up in the blog, then he must have some unusual quirk or character flaw that would make him wary. Therefore, he could potentially weed himself out of the mix. I mean, really, if a date doesn't think these stories are as crazy and off the wall as I do, there may be a problem. See? It is a screening tool.

On the other hand, if I told people who didn't know me, it could foster a sense of insecurity. They may not know that I would never write about someone who is my friend. I would never write about someone who is nice and normal that just didn't work out. I would never embellish or make these things up. Because, really, who could make this stuff up? Certainly not me. But still, could be a scare tactic.

I came to the conclusion that a pen name was not necessary. It's not like I was a household name. But I do think the decision to tell men had to be made judiciously. So I decided: Screening Tool AND Scare Tactic.

The Married Guy Update

I never thought I would say this, but there was a married guy update. One would think that after my particular dating history I would be hard to surprise, yet I found that I was surprised every time something weird or bad happened. And good things really threw me for a loop.

I think the married guy was at least a year or two before this update. Remember, I never talked to the guy, met him, nothing. Then I had the very unusual email conversation with the wife who caught him on the dating site. So fast-forward two years, and I get an email from Married Guy asking me to "share" on Yahoo. I didn't use my Yahoo account, so I was not sure what that meant. I decided it was a good time to delete that email address!

I guess the wife's "plan" to catch him on the dating site failed if she was even still with him. I have to admit, this sparked some curiosity in me about what her plan was and if she followed through with it. I was not curious enough, however, to "share" with the guy. My guess would be that she was still with him. After all, he had cheated before and rather than leave him she decided she would make a "plan" to catch him in the act. The other scenario could be that the wife sent the sharing invitation to see if he was still in communication with me. I wouldn't put that past her since she seemed to be a plan-hatcher. The third option was that he sent out a mass invitation to this share thing and was too stupid to delete my address when wifey caught him. This was probably the most likely scenario, but deliberate intent could not be ruled out.

Regardless of the scenario, I was annoyed. If he were still at it--cyber-cheating--then leave me out of it. Gross, yuk, spit. If it were the wife, she was certifiable. If he sent some mass invite, then have the decency and respect for the wife and for me to have deleted me when you were found out the last time.

After all the yuckiness of dating I have experienced in the last few years, I have never been a "man-hater." I have not gotten bitter or cynical or jaded. And believe me, at times this has taken effort. I believed there were good and decent people out there. I think I even knew a few. But men like Married Guy made that effort harder.

So dude, grab some morality and be on your way!

BFD

Category 1: Those Who Fail to Embrace Their Own Reality.

Category 2: Liar, Liar Pants on Fire.

Category 3: Too Much Too Fast .

Dating Tips:

1. *If a guy/girl has only one photo and it is from the shoulders up, be prepared for anything.*
2. *If you are not interested, say so. This goes for men and women. The alternative of making someone wonder is just plain cruel. As I say, we are not in high school anymore.*
   a. *Example: Thank you so much for the nice dinner. I just don't think we are a good fit. [See how this makes it not personal? No criticism, no list of faults. Easy peasy.*
3. *Follow your own rules.*
4. *Don't ride in the car with someone on the first date.*
5. *Don't go for a walk on the beach, or get in a boat, or go swimming alone with someone you don't know. Too easy to hide the body.*

BIG RED FLAG (Right off the bat and I totally missed it.)

BFD, poor guy. He **seemed normal.** Nice profile, decent picture. The picture was only a head shot, though. I am not the kind of girl that had to have a physically perfect guy. In fact, I would rather a guy be a little bigger than smaller. I also have known so many people, men and women, who become more and more attractive as you get to know them. And sometimes, the more you know someone, the less attractive they become. The outside can fade or change, but it is what is inside that matters. I really believed that.

BFD and I talked on the phone a couple of times. He seemed nice and normal. He was employed, had a house he was renovating, was close to his family. He enjoyed a nice glass of red wine and had friends come over for cook outs. These are all good things. He did say, "I am kind of chubby." I said, "Who cares, everyone goes up and down." And I meant that. We set a date and agreed to meet at a restaurant at the beach.

I got there first. As I was walking in from the parking lot, I saw him in his car rounding the lot looking for a parking spot. I waved and walked to the door to wait. The gravel waterfront parking lot was about 100 yards long and very narrow. He parked three-quarters of the way down, so when I saw him, I spotted him from the color of his burgundy shirt too far down the lot to see anything else. He was walking toward me. As he slowly came into focus, I thought, well, he is kind of chubby. He came closer. I thought, oh, well, he is quite chubby. As he finally came up the steps, I thought, okay, 400 pounds is more than a little chubby. He looked like someone had squeezed his legs and the body inflated like a big ball. He had also said he was over six feet tall. I think at one point he may have been.

But the curvature of his spine caused by the weight of his body rendered him well-below the six-foot mark.

At this point I felt a bit shallow. My internal dialogue was working overtime, telling myself what a heel I was, and I decided to give the guy a chance. He could be perfectly nice and smart and funny.

So I said hello and we walked up the steps to the restaurant. In Pensacola, waterfront restaurants are built up high to avoid water damage during storms. We walked up to the main level of the Grand Marlin. It was a popular Gulf-side restaurant that has an open-air deck with live music and a warm sea breeze. I introduced him to the army of friends that I bumped into (because in a smallish town like Pensacola, you can't go anywhere, especially on a Friday night, without bumping into 15 of your closest friends) while beginning the two-hour wait to eat. Luckily, he decided we should go somewhere downtown to avoid the wait. He decided I should just ride over the bridge with him so we didn't have to take two cars. I wasn't thrilled about riding in his car, but it was a short drive and I went with it. This little tidbit becomes important later.

We went to the Fish House, a popular place downtown that is also built up high and has an open-air deck, live music and sits on the water. There is nothing like coastal living. There was no wait this time, and again, I saluted the second wave of friends I saw there. We sat to eat at one of the long wooden outdoor booths. Once seated across from him, I looked up and noticed that his skin was gray. Really, really gray. Not like a guy-without-a-tan gray, but a sickly not-getting-enough-circulation gray. It was kind of pasty and made him look unhealthy. This was not good. My determination to give him a fair shot wavered.

We talked about the usual first date things. What you like to do for fun, places you go, etc. He told me he played tennis and loved the beach like me. Huh. Really? Mental pictures abound.

BIG RED FLAG

Then he mentioned that he had been married once and engaged twice since then. I understand that things happen. I am certainly not the one to judge failed relationships. But engaged twice and not married? Does he jump into the engagement too quickly? Is he making poor choices in women? Does he just want to get married and doesn't care to whom? Burning questions. And thus my wavering turned into full-fledged doubt.

The date was okay. We had a nice dinner at a nice restaurant. Conversation was okay. He asked questions and listened when I talked. He contributed to the conversation. This may not sound like much, but for some people, it's a resounding victory. I didn't laugh once. This was a disappointment. I needed someone funny, and I had this theory that humor is related to intelligence. I liked me some wit. And I kept going back in my mind to the tennis/beach comments. They just didn't ring true. I didn't believe that he actually got on a court and played tennis. At all. And I didn't see him taking long walks on the beach. Plus, I kept thinking that I had three boys. I needed someone who could keep up. We swam, we hiked, we played outside, we biked. I couldn't have some gray guy lagging behind. Ugh, I felt like a heel!

It was about ten pm by the end of dinner. He drove me back to my car at the first restaurant on the beach. He kept asking me to take a walk on the beach. As a general rule, I did not walk on the beach at night with strange men on a first date. [See, I followed my own rule!] That was just asking for trouble. Besides, his health was a serious concern to me. I didn't want to be trapped alone on the beach with him and have some health issue occur. I told him it was late and I had to go relieve the babysitter. He pulled into the parking lot next to my car. Before I could make a gentle exit, he leaned over to get my hair out of my face.

Oh crap, he had a move!

Then, before I knew it, he leaned in and kissed me. I had tried to have an open mind, but clearly I was not attracted to him. I did not see that coming. And when you do not want to kiss someone, you DO NOT want to kiss someone. As quickly and gracefully as I could, I said thank you for the date, my kids are waiting, and drive carefully. (See, I told you the riding in one car was significant and follow your own rule, you idiot.)

As I walked in the door at home about 15 minutes later, he called. I was paying the sitter and didn't answer. He asked me to let him know I made it home. I appreciated that. I think that is a sweet thing when guys do that. I texted him back to say I did and thanks for the date. He wrote back, *"That was a great date. That was a great kiss. We need to do that again soon."*

Ugh!

BIG RED FLAG

The next day, I sent him an email. I said, "Thank you so much for the date, but I don't think we are a good fit." This sentence is your friend, use it often.

He wrote back, *"That's really too bad. I thought we had a future."*

60

Ahhhh! Ha! This explained the serial engagements. A future after one date. Really? As I have said before, when I am on a first date I am just trying to decide if there should be a second date.

At some point, I decided to look at his online profile again. The online site gives options for you to list your body type. The options are: slender, about average, athletic and toned, curvy, need to shed a few and heavy set. BFD chose about average. A fatal error in embracing his own reality. How in the world did he come to that conclusion? Did he live with giants? Was his whole family morbidly obese, so this was normal in his world? I couldn't imagine.

As these things were reeling in my mind, I called my sister. I was feeling really bad for my thoughts. She made me feel tons better. She said that to get to the point where you are that big and that gray, you have to reach an extreme behavior. She related it to anorexia. That is an extreme problem related as much to mental as physical and she said he had to have an extreme part of his personality to get to that point. Phew! I felt better. She was right.

BFD was a little weird after my last email. He continued to write to me about once a week. I never wrote back because I didn't really have anything to add. This is an important philosophy. Don't go back, don't lead people on and don't drag it out when you know you are not interested. Nothing good will come of that. I had told him my thoughts and that was it. I had also learned through the stalker guy and the ex-husband that the best thing to do with extreme people is not to engage. It just makes it harder to disengage. He wrote for about two months, texted and called. It began to feel a little creepy. My sister was very, very right about the extreme thing.

During the two months of post The-End (in my mind) writing, my friend Laura called and said, "BFD tried to friend me on Facebook!"

"Who?" I didn't know who in the world she was talking about.

"BFD! Your big fat date!"

Sheesh!

And then my friend Tara called and said, "BFD tried to contact me on a dating site, and I have a picture of you and me on my profile!"

Let me just say, guys, do not contact girls who are friends of the girls you have met on dating sites. I am pretty sure this is not normal. I was to the point of getting worried.

But he finally got the hint and stopped.

The Toothless Guys (yes, that is plural)

Category 1: Those Who Are Not Ready to Date.

Category 2: Those Who Fail To Embrace Their Own Reality.

Category 3: Liar, Liar Pants on Fire.

Dating Tips:

1. *Don't date guys with missing teeth. Do I even need to say that?*
2. *Don't ask anyone out if you are missing teeth. Things that go without saying? One would think.*

I still have a hard time getting over the fact that I have a blog entry entitled, "The Toothless Guys." I could have called it "The Parade of Toothless Men." As dating goes, good teeth have always been big with me, but the presence of all teeth was not something I thought I needed to articulate as a requirement. I was wrong.

There were at least three or four dates with gaping holes. It is a funny thing that happens when you realize a date is missing teeth. There is the precise moment when he forgets and smiles too big or in some cases just opens his mouth to speak. A shiver goes through your whole body...and not the good kind of shiver. Once you see it, you know the flash of panic probably has shown on your face, and you hold your breath hoping he didn't notice you notice the absence of his choppers. The rest of the date is spent trying not to look at the empty space that seems to shout at you from his mouth. Try as you might, you can't stop looking. Torture, I tell you.

Two toothless dates stand out in my mind. There were more, but do I really need to belabor the point?

The First

He was one of my very first online dates ever. He was tall, oddly so, at 6'6". We went to the Melting Pot, a fondue restaurant for those of you who haven't been...fun and different. I never eat there. He was sweet. I found out later he still lived with his mother. Sweet or weird? A topic for another day; however, this could have been a **Big Red Flag.** The toothless thing just renders it irrelevant. He met me out in front of the restaurant, and I guess because of the enormity of him, I was chest level and couldn't see well enough at first to notice the mouth. We wound through the dimly-lit restaurant to a table off the beaten path. When we got to the table, he had flowers waiting for me. Now this was sweet, maybe a little much for a first date, but still. I had never dated anyone that was a flower giver...I think the ex-husband gave them maybe twice in 11 years. Nice so far.

We sat down and he was very shy and nervous. He struggled to find words and kept wiping his hands on his pants.

He opened his mouth to speak. I have no idea what he said because THE MOMENT had arrived. Half of the top tooth in the very front was missing. It was not like part of it had cracked off across. It was missing lengthwise. It was skinny. Oh no! And I couldn't stop looking. It was actually kind of mesmerizing because I couldn't get my mind out of this loop thinking, Why? How? Why? How?

The Second

This guy was an engineer. We met for lunch at a local soup and sandwich place where you stand in line to order and carry your food to the table. They had daily soups and sandwiches on a chalk board. As we were standing in line to place our orders, I thought he was nice. I was thinking that he looked like his picture, maybe even a little better, and then WHAMO! There it was. He smiled too much and there was the hole. At least his was further back, but he was missing his first molar on the bottom on one side. As we stood there, all I could think was, "Buddy, we should just save your money and go." I thought that would be mean, so I stayed. The good news was that we had nothing in common. He was only able to talk about surfing and cycling. Since I have little to no experience with either of these things, conversation was strained. Especially since he didn't seem to notice I had nothing to contribute about these topics. He also had a quirk of not being able to look at me while he was talking. That was odd. I kept thinking he either had social issues, or he couldn't stand the sight of me. I decided to go with the social issues line of thinking.

Deal Breakers

I have to say that both of these guys had jobs. Decent jobs. I feel pretty safe in thinking there was not a financial limitation that kept them from fixing the offending spaces. This meant that good teeth were not a priority in their lives. Deal breaker. And if either had an appointment to fix the gaping hole, the first thing out of their mouths should have been that they knew teeth were missing and they were on their way to the dentist. Better yet, they could have postponed the date. There's an idea!

I really haven't come up with a **BIG RED FLAG** for these guys. The only trick is that in their online dating photos, they are not smiling. I guess that counts. I do feel a need to go into a little bit more detail with their categories. So I will explain.

Category 1: Those Who Are Not Ready to Date.

In my mind, the toothless are not ready to date. This is a priority issue and it should be a priority to have all of your teeth. Until you reach this epiphany in life, don't date.

Category 2: Those Who Fail to Embrace Their Own Reality.

This is pretty obvious, don't you think? If you fail to recognize that toothlessness is not a way to woo a woman, you are not embracing your own reality.

Category 3: Liar Liar Pants on Fire.

Not smiling or keeping your mouth closed in a profile photo in order to hide gaping holes constitutes a lie in my book! Fix those choppers and smile for the camera!

The Guy Who Thinks He Likes Women, But Really He Doesn't

Category 1: Those who are not ready to date.

Category 2: Those who should just keep their own company.

Category 3: Those who think their profiles are witty and cute, but really they are not.

The good news about my never-ending email inbox was that I never deleted anything. In going through older emails, I came across this guy from an online dating site. He seemed to talk a lot about his life lessons, tried to sound evolved. By the way, trying too hard to seem anything is a **BIG RED FLAG.** But if you read between the lines, he had some issues. One of my biggest pet peeves in a profile was one in which a man listed all of the things he didn't want or didn't like or wished he hadn't experienced. This kind of list screams, "I AM NOT READY TO DATE!" Surely he was not over whatever happened in his last relationship. He was recently divorced or broken up or he had stellar grudge-holding fortitude.

BIG RED FLAGS

I saved this profile because it exemplifies the kind of profile I am talking about. This guy wrote a little better than the average guy who literally makes a list of things he hates. This guy weaved it into a paragraph that described his evolution of lessons in life, but really it was a more subtle slamming of women...or maybe a particular woman, who knows? And he ended with a bang giving a "toast" to the "nice guys." The funny thing about this toast was that his profile was not meant to be read by men. It was meant to attract women to date. So underneath his vitriol, he was using this tool to write about his supreme dislike of women. He just wanted a platform and an audience of women...so he could bash them. And I think we all know the word for that.

I knew that I couldn't effectively relate the details. So here it is verbatim:

I've learned that, no matter what happens, how bad it seems today, life does go on, and it will be better tomorrow. I've learned that you can tell a lot about a person by the way he/she handles four things: a rainy day, the elderly, lost luggage, and tangled Christmas tree lights. I've learned that, regardless of your relationship with your parents, you'll miss them when they're gone from your life. I've learned that making a 'living' is not the same thing as making a 'life..' I've learned that life sometimes gives you a second chance. I've learned that you shouldn't go through life with a catcher's mitt on both hands. You need to be able to throw something back. I've learned that if you pursue happiness, it will elude you. But if you focus on your family, your friends, the needs of others, your work and doing the very best you can, happiness will find you. I've learned that whenever I decide something with an open heart, I usually make the right decision. I've learned that even when I have pains, I don't have to be one. I've learned that every day, you should reach out and touch someone. People love that human touch -- holding hands, a warm hug, or just a friendly pat on the back. I've learned that I still have a lot to learn!

My Interjection

From this first paragraph, we have learned a few things. The guy had a rough break up, he had a difficult relationship with his parents, he needs a second chance, he was a taker not a giver, and he used to be a pain. We also know that he loves a good cliché. All of this from the first paragraph. Reading on...

I am not from here and do not suffer the attitude of those that are. I grew up in Southern California where you treat people with respect.

My Interjection

So, he doesn't like people from Pensacola (that already makes someone like me, from Pensacola, feel defensive...well, if you invest in the random profile). And what exactly is the attitude of those from here? If you are going to be insulting, don't be vague.

I spend every moment I can with my children, They are very important to me and they will always come first. You must understand that this is the way it is, and should always be. I would hope that you feel the same way about yours.

My Interjection

This sounds like a quality you would want in a man: one who cared for his children. But the tone of this comment makes you feel like he thinks your children aren't as important to you as his are to him. Off-putting to say the least. I wanted to stop reading now....but here we go!

I workout at the gym three days a week, more if I can.

My Interjection

This is one of those online "codes." It translates to "no fatties need apply." Don't fall for it.

I have a great job that I love. I really enjoy the people that I work with and for.

I love to dance, looking for someone who does as well, or is at least willing to take swing or ballroom dancing classes with me. I can fake it really well; however i believe it is beautiful and very sexy to dance with the one you love and to show off.

My Interjection

This is actually the least offensive and most normal statement in the whole post. Mostly because it is benign.

Everything I have I own. Except my apartment, it is adequate for my needs at the moment.

I am very outgoing and always open to new things. I enjoy the outdoors and would prefer to be at the park with my dog or fishing with my kids.

I am very shy when it comes to meeting people especially if I am attracted to them.

I enjoy being proud of the woman I am with and there is nothing sexier than being able to say, "Ya she is with me".

My Interjection

I would hope you own your stuff. I don't know why you would point this out. Has he been a frequent member of Rent-A-Center? I have no problem with that, but I don't think this is an attribute. As for renting his apartment that is adequate for his needs at the moment...well, I am not sure what he is trying to say there, but that feels like some kind of innuendo. And "Ya she is with me?" Ya? I can't even talk about that. Now we get to the toast.

THE NICE GUY!

*This is a tribute to the nice guys. The nice guys that finish last, that never become more than friends, that endure hours of whining and ****ing about what ***holes guys are [*remember, he is trying to pick up women*], while disproving the very point. This is dedicated to those guys who always provide a shoulder to lean on but restrain themselves to tentative hugs, those guys who hold open doors and give*

71

reassuring pats on the back and sit patiently outside the changing room at department stores. This is in honor of the guys that obligingly reiterate how cute/beautiful/smart/funny/sexy their female friends are at the appropriate moment, because they know most girls need that litany of support. This is in honor of the guys with open minds, with laid-back attitudes, with honest concern. This is in honor of the guys who respect a girls every facet, from her privacy to her theology to her clothing style. This is for the guys who escort their drunk, bewildered female friends back from parties and never take advantage once they're at her door [seriously???], for the guys who accompany girls to bars as buffers against the rest of the creepy male population.

My Final Thoughts

The toast. It should be called the Roast. He thinks women in general are whining bitchy things who complain and don't know what they want. His ex was apparently a big shopper who used him as a personal clothing rack. She was incredibly insecure and, therefore, apparently **all** women need a "litany of support." See what a giver he is? And he protects his drunk chicks…and doesn't even take advantage of them. Is that supposed to be a gift? Really? It's noble that he doesn't participate in what is basically date rape? Because it would be so easy to just go for it? I could go on and on. I just need a moment to breathe. What a guy!

I would like to give this poor fellow some advice. Please wait until you are over your misery. Until you are, you will not attract anyone. Everyone just out of a relationship thinks he/she is ready to date, and believe me, it is a rare occurrence when that is true. You have to learn to discern that one person does not a generalization make. And by all means, if you resent not taking advantage of your drunk, platonic girlfriends, please, for the love of God, seek counseling. Until you are past gross generalization, you are not ready to date. If women are such hard work and such a big drain on all of your patience and moral support, you are better off keeping your own company for a while.

When you begin to feel hopeful and optimistic, try, try again!

Mr. Smooth AKA The Guyzillian

Category 1: Those who were never ready to date.
Category 2: The guys your dad warned you about.
(With those two categories, who needs another?)

There was very little that put me over the edge into the "I give up" mentality. This one may have just pushed me into an extended dating break. I had one date with Mr. Smooth. We had spoken on the phone a couple of times and we texted for a couple of days. We met at 600 South, a local wine bar where you don't feel like the oldest one there at age 35. It is quiet, dimly lit, and the wait staff speaks in hushed tones. We were there for a couple of hours. He looked like his photo, big deal. He had all his teeth, woohoo. He could carry on a conversation, blah, blah, blah. There was no real connection. It was just a flat, blah date. It felt like he had been on a zillion first dates and was going down a rote list of socially acceptable questions with no real interest in the answers. Where do you work? Do you like it? Do you get along with your family? Do you have any siblings? When I tried to make conversation, I got one-word answers. It was like time was stalled and I didn't know how to escape. When he said he had an early morning at work and needed to get to bed early, I was thrilled. Finally, an exciting part of the date! I had no real desire to see him again and I was pretty sure he wasn't interested in seeing me again. So, the end.

And this is a total aside, but he had no lips. It was distracting. No lips to the point where I sat there thinking, how does someone have no lips whatsoever?

Another aside, we were talking about politics and he used the words, "Barack Hussein Obama." That was really the end for me. I can't stand it when people feel compelled to insert the middle name. There is an implication there that I can't tolerate.

At the end of the date, he said, *"'Bye."* I said , "'Bye." There were no plans made, no "I'll call you," or "let's do this again." Fine by me. Not a bad date, just blah. I didn't hear from him for two days. I didn't even notice. Normally after a decent date, I tend to think, "Huh, that guy never called. I wonder why." Little chip at the self-esteem. This time, didn't even notice. It wouldn't even have been blog-worthy except....

Two days later, I got a text. I am going to type the conversation verbatim. Turns out, he was VERY, VERY blog worthy.

Mr. Smooth: *Hey.*

Me: Hey

Mr. Smooth: *Whatcha doin*

Me: Just finished a movie

Mr. Smooth: *Ahhhh, I just got in from sailing*

Mr. Smooth: *The tenderness has finally gone away lol*

[At this point I don't know what he is talking about, but I went along with it thinking maybe I forgot something he had told me.]

Me: That's good!

Mr. Smooth: Completely functional now :)

Me: What a relief.

[Now I am thinking, he's not really going there, is he? Can't be!]

Mr. Smooth: I know! I was worried.

Me: :)

Mr. Smooth: Well, in theory

Me: Theory?

Mr. Smooth: You could borrow it, but you probably have toys so wouldn't need it.

[Uh-oh. He really isn't going there? Please don't!]

Mr. Smooth: Ummmm my smooth c!@# and balls lol, thanks for making me say it

[Crap, at this point I remember that that week he had gone to the spa. He told me he was going to get a "guyzillian wax." This is something you put out of your mind forever. I was not thrilled it was resurrected. I thought he was joking. Apparently not.]

Me: What?

Mr. Smooth: Huh?

Me: I am confused. Are you sure you meant to write to me?

[I thought maybe he had an inappropriate conversation going with someone else and maybe he didn't know he was writing to me.]

Mr. Smooth: lol yes. Blame it on the full moon.

Me: Are you drunk?

Mr. Smooth: A tad

Mr. Smooth: But more horny than drunk:)

Me: Ok. This is a big leap from 600 South (first-date wine bar where he was the most boring and least conversational date to that point).

Mr. Smooth: Wanna leap?

Me: Maybe you should sleep it off.

Mr. Smooth: I've only had two

Me: You said you were a lightweight :) (This I remembered from the first date…how could this even be the same guy?)

Mr. Smooth: Haha, I am

Me: Do you normally have a glass of wine with someone and then take a leap?

Mr. Smooth: What's your favorite position?

Me: Seriously. Too much. I don't know you at all.

Mr. Smooth: I'm trying to get to know you. And no I don't, it's been a while.

Mr. Smooth: How long has it been for you? I just figured we liked each other.

Me: I don't talk sex with someone I've met once.

Mr. Smooth: Twice?

Me: No thanks, bye.

Mr. Smooth: Bye

Enough said.

The Attitude

Online dating can be fun...or it can be miserable. It's all in the attitude you take. You must recognize and accept all of the possibilities--the good, the bad and the eye-roll inducing. I am not telling you my stories to steer you clear of online dating. I know this may not seem like the case. I am telling you about them because they are funny, you will probably relate to them and you can certainly learn from them. Once you have the right attitude, online dating can be very entertaining. And maybe even satisfying.

The first step to successful online dating is to have realistic expectations. First of all, do not go into a first date expecting him to be your one and only. You expect that this is a first date. You even expect that it may be the last date with that person. I don't care how well your emailing, texting and phone calling have been going, sometimes when you meet someone in person, it does not meet the expectations you have set based on your previous communication. You may have no physical attraction. There may be a discrepancy between what you thought and what is. If you go in expecting this to be the beginning of a wonderful, long-term relationship, you are bitterly disappointed if it isn't and thus you are on the rollercoaster. Save yourself from these dramatic ups and downs –the certainty of knowing this is IT! Followed by the devastation of realizing, no it's NOT!

If you have a good or even great first date, yea! Make a second date. Still follow the same rule from above. Everyone is on their best behavior in the early I-really-want-you-to-like-me stages of dating. This is normal. What is not normal (remember BFD…"I thought we had a future") is when you fail to recognize the too-much-too-fast syndrome in yourself. For some reason, this is so much easier to spot in others. Dating is a process, not an event. Take it one date at a time and let it grow at a natural pace. There is no timeframe for changing your Facebook status to "in a relationship."

The second rule in online dating is to embrace a healthy perspective. This one can be tough. When a date doesn't work out because someone decides he doesn't want to date you, it is not fun. It feels like rejection or criticism. You know the sentiment I used repeatedly to end communication? "Thank you so much for the date, but I just don't think we are a good fit"? Well, it applies to you, too. If someone uses it on you, be thankful that he let you know it wasn't what he was looking for and move on. Now, I can't guarantee that everyone has learned this handy little phrase, so if he bungles it, you can feel free to suggest that he borrow this little gem in the future.

The third rule is to embrace your own reality. If you have a bad date, well, it's not the end of the world. Move on. If you have a date that is just mediocre, you have two choices: give the benefit of the doubt and try again or move on. I believe that the benefit of the doubt approach should be used sparingly. Most of the time your first instinct is correct, but every now and then there may be a reason things aren't exactly right. If one of you is tired, sick or had a particularly bad day, you may need a do-over if all other signs point to possibilities. If you had a bad date, then by all means move on. Embrace that your date was less than perfect, use your handy exit line and don't look back. If you get rejected, do not take it personally. I repeat…DO NOT TAKE IT PERSONALLY.

The reason people date is to find out if you are compatible. The fact that you are not does not indicate any flaw in you whatsoever. It indicates that you are not a good match. This is okay. This is normal. Think about it--statistically, you will not be a good fit with most of your dates. This is why dating isn't easy. If you accept this premise, then you accept that dating is a process, not an event, and you can enjoy it. Good or bad. And you can realize that a rejection is a good thing. It means you won't end up with the wrong person. Because remember our mantra?

Our mantra is the final rule. Let's say it together: I would rather be alone for the rest of my life than be with the wrong person. This mantra helps you to avoid settling. It means you will not think someone is better than no one. It helps you avoid thinking you can fix someone. You can't. End of story. And if you try, you will fail. Because you can't.

If someone professes a willingness to change, wait until said change has been accomplished before dating. Because you will be resented for this change if you are in even remote proximity. The real final rule is that you need to find a whole person. Someone who has dealt with the issues and the baggage and arrived at a whole, healthy, happy place all by themselves. At that point, you can say, "I would rather be with you than anyone else on the planet." When you can say that…without reservation…without condition…without any buts….well, then you are ready.

The Wanna Shoot My Gun Guy

Category 1: Guys who just aren't right for you.

Dating Tips:

1. Lunch-hour dates are a good idea.
2. Never go to someone's house if you do not know them.

This poor fellow. He **seemed normal.**..in a sweet and childish sort of way. We met for coffee at Starbucks during my lunch hour from work. Lunch-hour dates, by the way, are a good idea if you are meeting someone you don't know... for obvious reasons. It is limited by time. You have a built-in excuse to leave if it's a disaster. And you can get along with anyone for an hour, right?

Anyway, he was right on time. Check. Looked like his picture. Check. He was nice and polite. Check. On the right track so far? Sure.

He began the date by telling me how he used his new GPS to get to Starbucks. He lived in Milton, a "suburb" of Pensacola. Milton is not that far and is basically a part of Pensacola, so needing a GPS to get to Pensacola proper is slightly hilarious. When he found out I didn't have one, he started talking about getting me a GPS for Christmas. This was sweet. He was very sweet, but this was incredibly premature considering Christmas was three months away. Could he be of the "too much too fast" persuasion?

The more he talked the more I realized that he was, in fact, sweet, but very simple. He asked me what a word that I used meant. I wish I could think of the word, but I can't. I thought that was a bit funny, but when he started to tell me how when he read a book, he had to keep a dictionary at hand, I thought, "uh-oh." I guess he wasn't a big fan of discerning meaning from context? I'm not sure I would admit that on a first date, but who knows?

The interesting thing was that he had a degree and was working on his masters. He said it took him a long time to do it, but he was determined. I think his determination is admirable. Most people do not pursue things that are difficult. So he had character.

The short and sweet coffee date went fine, but he was probably not for me. The next day he called and wanted to plan a date for the weekend.

BIG RED FLAG

"You could come to my house. Wanna shoot my gun? We could shoot cans off the porch rail."

Okay. The mind reels. First, this was not the follow-up date proposal I expected from my little dictionary-using, GPS-wielding guy who oozed sweetness. Second, there is no going to someone's house that you don't know. We all know about "The Criminal," right? Third, if any other man had asked me if I wanted to "shoot his gun," my mind probably would have taken it as innuendo. We all know about "Big Frank," right? And finally, really? Really? He invited me for a gun date?

There are no words. I used my old friend: Thank you so much for the coffee date, but I do not think we are a good fit. Someone said I should be careful because he may toss me in the river with the cement blocks holding up his car.

It does create quite a mental picture, doesn't it?

The Way Out

In all of my experiences with bad dates, I have realized that one of the hardest things to do is to let someone know that you are not interested in seeing them again, especially if they want to see you. I have friends who will actually accept multiple dates in order not to have to "hurt someone's feelings." I know some people that think that everyone has "issues" and you have to learn to work with what you've got. I am of the mind that if you see a trait that is a deal breaker for you, the deal breaker must actually break the deal.

Shall I say it again? Because this is REALLY important.

The deal breaker must actually break the deal.

To me there is no more dishonest way to lead someone on than to allow him to believe that you are interested when you are not. How would you feel if someone went out with you, not because he liked you, but because he didn't want to hurt your feelings? I'll tell you how you would feel – pathetic! No one wants that. You are not doing anyone any favors, and the longer you let it go on (I have seen friends let this go on for years…I am not kidding…years) the harder you make it on yourself to exit gracefully.

I guess this thought process is how I became known as the one-date-wonder to many of my friends. I was good at spotting qualities in a guy that I knew were not for me. Some were obvious (think "The Criminal," "Sweeten the Deal," etc.). Some were less obvious such as people who lacked a sense of humor or the ability to understand sarcasm. The key is to know your own mind and what you do and do not want. And to be okay with that knowledge. Standards are good. Settling is bad. Simple as that.

The ability to recognize my deal breakers prompted the problem of learning how to let someone know that I didn't want another date. I had to find a way of saying it that was benign and kind, but definitely got the message across. Let me introduce you to my handy little way out: "Thank you so much for a nice date. I really enjoyed meeting you, but I don't think we are a good fit." Write this down and use it often.

Perfect, right? Early in an online/phone/texting/dating relationship, there is no reason to go into any detail about why you don't want to go out. At this point, all you owe anyone is that the status of your interest has changed. Most people will accept this as a way out. Some will ask for reasons or details about what you are thinking. Do not succumb to the temptation to spill your guts. Making a list of flaws only serves to hurt and belittle. Do not get sucked into any more explanation because it will not go well. So many people want a list of reasons why you don't want to date them. After only a date or two or even three, this is not necessary and, in fact, can be cruel. The fact is, just because this person may not be right for you, does not mean he isn't right for someone else. If we all learned to take the fact that someone doesn't want to date us as a decision that we are not compatible rather than a personal affront, then our self-esteem would be in such better shape!

The Ultimate Run-on!

Category 1: Those who DO possess self-awareness.
Category 2: Those who are just not right for you.

Dating Tips

1. *Appreciate people for who they are, even if they are just not right for you.*

Imagine my delight at the receipt of the following email:

I came across your profile and although we might not be a match I thought you might want a laugh
so if you have a minute please read my profile and add criticism wherever it may need some
I do appreciate your opinion and comments
thanks (name withheld for his own protection)
P.S. I do think you pretty hot also

And yes, the lack of punctuation, among other things, is an indication of things to come...please enjoy his profile. I just had to share. Enjoy:

large teddy bare, tattooed ex biker that doesn't ride anymore and that's only cause I don't have a bike right now I am disabled! it's a legs thing so you know I'm on SSI so I don't make a lot of money but that shouldn't be important in a relationship but I do all right I don't play games ever!!! And I hate drama so I wont give you any I know I look like I'm mean as hell but just the opposite is true I'm a pushover to the right people I'm a lover not a fighter[had enough of that crap in my life] love the beach, new places, home were ever that may be and some kids not the hyper or obnoxious ones just the good ones JUST KIDDING I do have a scene of hummer I likes intimate relationship I will let you know you are appreciate you and I will do anything I can for you I'd like to meet someone special a little mouthy is OK and if you don't mind an older dude I'd love to have you to fill that void in my life if you would like to live in the Pensacola area or I can be talked in to moving but I love the beach! No drama no bipolar BS or wild ass chicks!! what a minute strike the wild ass chick thing there OK to just want to live and love like life should be OK back to me!!!! WORNING I DO HAVE A MOUTH ON ME AND I UES IT! I cook, clean, I can separate whites from colored close and actually get them washed, folded and put away I can fix just about anything, I know I will never win a fight with a woman, as in there's no point if we need to fight we don't need each other Ha here's a bad joke! if a woman bitches and a man isn't around to hear it does that make her still wrong??? OK I warned you it was bad OK I know the toilet seat goes down for some strange reason I haven't figured out yet, And I'm house broken!!! I don't need to be told a thousand times to get off my ass and do something for you! once will do just fine I will do it, I love kids but not cartoons unless it's family guy or something along that lines huge fan of syfi I would say my friends don't come over and BBQ, get drunk and make a mess but I think we both know that wouldn't be true so I wont push my luck I will promise to do the best I can to make you happy, feel loved and appreciated and I know it takes two to take care of a house and that mean a 50/50 deal!!!!!

There are several things that Mr. Run-On Sentence has going for him. One, he has self-awareness enough to know that we are not a good fit. I didn't even have to tell him! Score one for him! Second, he has enough self-awareness to know that his profile may have a mistake or two. He's on a roll! Three, he gave me a compliment, so he is making an effort. That is just being nice.

The thing that he doesn't quite realize is that his profile didn't need any help from me. As I said in the previous chapter, just because a guy isn't a good fit for me doesn't mean that he isn't perfect for someone else. There is someone out there perfect for Mr. Run-On. And that is why he should leave his profile just the way it is. There is truth in advertising and like attracts like. For me to have given him pointers would have been to change who he is (on paper). I think your profile should be an accurate reflection of who you are and the way you think and speak and spell. The fact that he and I are not a good fit is not a reflection on either of us.

It just is the way it is.

Elizabeth Denham

Writing a Great Profile

I think now is a good time to talk about what makes a good profile. I am wondering how many I have read in more than five years of online dating. It has to be in the thousands. In reading so many, I have laughed, wanted to cry, been entertained, horrified and sometimes perplexed. There are a few common elements that have made me want to respond to someone's profile as well as a few trends that make me want to run far, far away.

Things That Make People Want to Respond

One of the first things necessary to a good profile is honesty. If you lie about your looks, height or weight you are setting yourself up to let someone down. The worst feeling in the world, I would think, is to see a disappointed look on someone's face at the sight of you. Not to mention, whether or not you believe the physical things don't matter (because, yes, I know, it's what's on the inside that matters) it is still a lie. And if you are not ready to own who you are, including how you look, you might want to think about accomplishing that ownership before you date. If you lie about other things such as education, income, smoking, and drinking, you are a liar. It doesn't matter how small the lie, one little lie can cast doubt in your date's mind that can undermine a relationship before it even starts. And starting off with a lie is a deal breaker for me and I would hope for most everyone.

Now, I am not saying that to avoid lying you must share every detail of your life. This brings me to the next quality of a good profile: Don't over share. You don't need to give your life story. Secrets must be earned by the evolution of a friendship, not revealed out of some false sense of obligation. Share enough in your profile to pique someone's interest, but don't share details of your divorce, problems of your childhood, etc.

When trying to come up with the body of your profile, do your best to write like you speak. I know it isn't necessarily the easiest thing to do, but if you can come close, it will give your potential dates a sense of your personality. Include a philosophy that you have about life, the things you are interested in, something funny or quirky. You should also include what you have to offer as much as what you want. It is, after all, as much about your date as it is about you. Many profile writers miss this mark.

Be sure to include a variety of photos from head shots to full-body pictures. Also make sure they are recent. It can be a good idea to update them periodically, as it shows people you are adding recent photos and that you are actively participating on the dating site. This lends to the honesty characteristic mentioned above and attracts more potentials.

Have a good tag line. This is the introductory line at the top of the profile. Avoid the cheesy (Prince Charming looking for his Snow White) and avoid making a joke no one else will understand. Inside jokes don't work if you are the only one in on it. This is not as easy as it sounds, so experiment with a few and see what you come up with!

Things That Make People Want to Run Away

Never, ever, ever make a list of qualities that you do not want and include them in your profile. It is negative. You want to be a positive and attractive personality. You don't want to make someone afraid of having their qualities ticked off a list. Once you decide you want to go out with someone, there are conversational questions you can ask to deduce if there are deal breakers present.

Also, steer clear of having a list of the type of person for whom you are looking. This kind of list keeps people from responding who don't think they meet those particular criteria but might be great people. Not only that, but you are locking yourself into a "type." Limiting your options and sticking with a type is just a bad idea. And apparently hasn't worked out so far, has it? Know your deal breakers but otherwise, keep your options open. You could end up with someone unexpected!

Do not include self-portraits on your profile. This includes, for both men and women, photos taken in the bathroom mirror, in your car or at your desk at work. No one's arm is long enough to take a great self-portrait and besides, it is almost impossible to get your own extended arm out of the photo. Find a friend, as embarrassing as it may be, and take a few good pictures. It will be worth it.

Do not use pictures of your boat, your car, your pet or your kids as your profile picture. No one knows how to read that and most people pass you by. The point of a profile picture is to get an idea of what YOU look like. Suck it up and put it out there.

Do not talk about your previous relationships or dates in your profile. No one reading about you wants to know what you think of those experiences as they are probably not happy and sunny or they wouldn't be in the past. Focus on your optimism for your potential dates and look forward.

Writing a profile is not an easy feat. Take your time with it and give it some real thought. This is, after all, your potential date's first impression of you. Once you publish it, don't feel locked into it. You can edit any time, and if people are asking you some of the same questions, maybe you can work that information into your profile. It can be a work in progress edited to reflect who you are as you evolve in the process of online dating.

Have fun with it and so will the people reading it!

Bubble Bath and a Glass of Wine?

Category 1: The cynical ones.

Dating Tips:

1. If someone judges your whole gender negatively, you are already starting off in a hole. Don't try to dig your way out of the flaws of half the world. Move on.

I have to disagree with the author of the profile below. He says it's not about bubble bath and a glass of wine anymore. It's about "email and how much I make." No, little dude, it's not about that either. It is about self-awareness. It's about knowing who you are and what you want and knowing who has enough in common with you to make something special (or just tolerate your quirks).

I have learned over the years that you have to be somewhat specific in your profile to identify what you want, and to some degree, what you don't. But I really detest it when people list the things that they can't stand in a profile. For example, people love to list a distaste for liars, cheaters and drama queens. I'm pretty sure everyone would love to eliminate that from potential dates. Online daters frequently request people without baggage. If you have managed to live to be older than 40 without it, then we all need to read your book! The bottom line is that these lists can make you sound like you are not over the last person who embodied these traits. A generic list of dislikes can truly go without saying. I do have to admit that I did finally add a line to my profile about my obsession with grammar. And, well, there is a part that says "If you have ever uttered the words 'it don't,' then I am not the girl for you." Living around here, it just needed to be said. I had to have a way of weeding that out. I cringe at the sound of those words, so really, I am saving people some trouble by admitting it outright.

So here is Mr. Negative's profile:

Hello im (name removed for his own protection) ,im an old fashioned kuntry man that still believes in true love and romance.

im an ex chef of 17 yrs,i love outdoor activities,all types of music except gangster rap,mostly into country music,i am spontanious and a pleaser but not a smotherin,controllin ass kisser...lol.i preferr a career woman with a mind of her own...i dont mind raisin kids but dnt need anymore girlfriends to raise...lol.

im a movie buff n enjoy a quiet night at home with a nice meal n a fire goin n snuggle up wh a good movie.im laid back and easy goin but not nieve.still a lil gun shy but i dnt believe in judging others from my past experiences,my heart has been broken ,can you fix it? p.s. im not in prison so i dnt need a pen pal,and dnt do 1 niterzz,"ONLY SERIOUS INQUIRIES ONLY NEED APPLY" ...lol!!!! Have you seen some of this stuff on here???? im not lookn for busty california girls,or hot single moms lookn for older single dads,or foriegn exchange students lookn to get legal...lmao...wow wht a trip..what happened to chivelry,n a lil romance.instead of a glass of wine and a bubble bath,now its all about e mail and how much i make...

First Date
I would like to wow you with my culinary skills with a nice meal and a fire and snuggle on the couch with good conversation and a movie....p.s.my fav movie is (the notebook). n "hell no" i aint gay...lol.

The thing is, any woman who went out with this man had a pretty big hurdle to overcome…his negative view of women on the whole. And I would caution any woman that any attempt to overcome this view and to prove him wrong about our gender is a daunting task and, really, not your job. Let him do the work he needs to do first. Then, let him rewrite his profile. Then, wait and see.

He sent me an email letting me know he liked my essay and asking if I were interested in a "good hearted kuntry man." Very sweet.

And pretty optimistic of him…

I am Speechless

Category 1: Those who think their profiles are witty and cute but really they are not.

Sometimes I come across a profile that simply must be shared. This is one of those. I am at a loss, really, as to how this one thinks he will get a date with all of his little "updates." We all know I have a thing about spelling and grammar, and this profile isn't quite up to par on that. But I really dislike it when people use text lingo in a profile. I guess with a username like "trickyazzz" there is nowhere to go but down.

I think my favorite line just might be, "that thing has a shelf life & im going to use it." You really and truly can't make this up. Please enjoy trickyazz in all of his glory.

UPDATE HERE WE GO AGAIN !!! if i have to add onemore update ,i think i give up !!! this is getting old ,if u cant give common respect & act like a adult .whats wrong with ppl wont show some resepect & reply --just say im not interested??? -ever heard of 10 fold ??? -treat others the way u want tobe treated ??? so when someone does it to u 10 times ,dont ask urself why ,its cus its same crap u done to someone else !!! go figure -ok sorry but if ur an idiot or bipolar or stuck on urself or dont reply back --then leave me alone !!!!

THINK I NEED TO MAKE A LIST WITH ALL THESE RUDE AZZ PPL ON IT , POST IT & LET OTHERS ADD TO IT !

put on ur seat belt ,,it could be a wild ride!!

lookin for my best friend, "one" good ole country girl, with some up top, curves are fine with me! thicker women welcome!! i understand life & we all change sooner or later, if u judge me before u know me, dont even talk to me, i dont need or want friends like that. im pretty laid back ,im blunt & open, say what you mean & mean what you say!! love music that has meaning, mostly rock like (shinedown,seether,tool,fuel,staind ,nickelback) love country food ,im a goof mostly, im high on life, love to laugh, but know when tobe serious. im happy go lucky , dont need anyone trying change my roll. i know what i want in life & have goals, i love racing (i drive dirt track late model car), 4 wheeling, active, anything fun, watch dvd, going to river with my english bulldogs, spending time with kids, they deserve to have good fresh start on life when they get older, always been family man, love kids, im self employed for 20 years ,love my job & its flexible, not into the party scene, i like to go out to clubs play pool,foosball, drink very little, no drugs, dont mind if someone else does. i dont like mean or rude people. likes sex (freak in the bed) ,that thing has a shelf life & im going to use it! hehe! i never judge book by its cover. i got my own money, home, truck. i dont use people, i got my own, dont like fighting, fussing, drama. people can shine if no one is holding them back or controlling them, cant never could do nothing, not into playing games,,theres not much trust, truth, or respect for others now days . i can live with anyone, but i want the one i cant live with out!!! if you have been treated bad in your past by others -i didnt do it! your past is old history -leave it in the past & look forward to the future! why be unhappy one more day! get over it! so if ya wanna chat, look me up, drop me a line ,apply within!

LOOKING for someone who is :: giving, simple things, wants tobe happy in life & has goals would be a plus. not controlling, that knows what family values & morals mean.. knows what agree to disagree means & never go to bed mad !! someone who can speak there opinin without being mad ,if i disagree!! someone funny, kind hearted, caring, respectful to others, good conversation ,COMMUNICATION is everything, someone who wants tobe treated right & knows how to return it!! a one sided deal will not work, it takes two on the same page to work thru life together, gotta start somewhere & see where it goes..but leave your past drama & history at the door!! if this is you, im game!!

UPDATE! (freak in the bed) MEANS THERES MANY OTHER OPTIONS THAN THE SAME OLE SAME OLE - GOTTA KEEP IT EXCITING ,OR LIFE GETS BORING ! CHANGE IT UP SOME, YOU MIGHT LIKE IT !

UPDATE! HERE WE GO! THIS MIGHT NOT BE GOOD -BUT IM GOIN TO SAY IT ANYWAY -I HAVE NOTHING AGAINST DIFFERENT SIZE OR COLOR WOMEN -THERES SOMEONE OUT THERE FOR EVERYBODY , MAYBE IM PICKY ,BUT I DO KNOW WHAT IM ATRACTED TOO ~ I LIKE THICK OR CHUNKY CURVY WOMEN WITH BRAINS, WITH BOOBS -SORRY THATS JUST WHAT I LIKE -I DIDNT WANT TO PUT IT OUT HERE LIKE THIS -BUT IT SEEMS

SOME PPL CANT READ OR DONT READ OR DONT UNDERSTAND WHAT THICK OR CHUNKY OR WITH BOOBS OR WITH BRAINS MEANS -SO GO ASK A FRIEND WHAT THEY THINK YOU ARE IF YOU DONT KNOW !!! -IM NOT TRYING TOBE A SMARTAZZZ HERE OR RUDE ,MEAN OR DEGRADE ANYBODY - BUT DAMMN WHERE DO THESE PEOPLE COME FROM, IF YOU CANT READ ,GO SLAP YO MAMA... HEHE! IM JUST SAYING WE ARE ALL DIFFERENT & WE HAVE THE RIGHT & A CHOICE OF WHAT WE LIKE ,AS WE ALL DO -BUT IF YOU GOIN TO HIDE THINGS -YOUR NOT READY TO EVEN MEET SOMEONE ! WE (WELL NOT SURE ABOUT EVERYBODY ELSE ,BUT SPEAKING FOR MYSELF.) IM HERE TRYING TO GET TO KNOW SOME NEW FRIENDS & GO FROM THERE !!! IF YOU CANT BE HONEST & SHOW SOME RESPECT ,KEEPING STEPIN !!! CUS I DONT EVEN WANT TO CHAT WITH SOMEONE HIDING THINGS -ALL I HEAR MOST TIME -IS IM TRYING OR WORKING ON LOSING MORE WEIGHT ! GUESS WHAT -I DONT CARE - I LIKE BIGGER WOMEN 160 TO 300 DEPENDS ON BUTT,BOOBS,HEIGHT & HEALTH -I LIKE BIG BOOBS & CURVES -LIKE A WOMAN THAT EATS & IS HAPPY , DAMMN THE BOITCHING -IM A HAPPY GO LUCKY ,FUN PERSON ,& IM GOING TO STAY THAT WAY - IF YOU DONT FIT OR I DONT FIT WHAT WE BOTH WANT ,LET THE OTHER PERSON KNOW -I KNOW YOU TALK TO SOME PPL & WONDER WHY THEY SO DAMMN RUDE -I DO -BUT GUESS WHAT IM NOT HERE TO CHANGE YOU -IM HERE TO MEET SOMEONE THATS ON SAME PAGE -RESPECT & COMMINCATION IS MY BIGGEST THINGS -BE OPEN -BE YOURSELF -WHY PUT ON A FRONT -YOU ARE WHO YOU

ARE -BUT IF I DO HAPPEN TO MEET YOU ,GUESS WHAT ITS NICE WHEN YOUR THE SAME PERSON OR LOOKS THE SAME AS IN PICTURES WHEN YOU MEET - PPL SEEM TO LIE ALOT !GO FIGURE !SO HAVE FEW DECENT PICTURES OF YOURSELF ~ WE ARE ALL DIFFERENT ,IN SHAPES, SIZES, COLORS,THOUGHTS,OPINIONS,SEX & TASTE ~ LIFE IS GOOD, LIFE IS FUN ,LIVE FREE, SMILE & BE HAPPY ~~OTHERS MIGHT NOTICE~~ MY MOTO IS: IF ITS NOT FUN ,IM NOT DOIN IT !

UPDATE! STOP WASTING MY TIME ! IF YOU NOT INTERESTED, SAY SO ,IF U DONT HAVE TIME SAY SO - LAST TIME I LOOKED ,THIS IS A ADULT SITE -WHICH MEANS SHOW SOME RESPECT TO OTHERS .. ~ JUST BE NICE & SAY IM NOT INTERESTED AT THIS TIME ~ SAY WHAT U MEAN & MEAN WHAT U SAY GEEZ! IF YOU WANT TO PLAY A GAME ,IM NOT INTERESTED ! -IF SOMEONE ASK YOU SOMETHING & YOU DONT REPLY ,THAT MEANS YOUR HIDING SOMETHING -I MEAN IF IM GOIN TO CHAT WITH YOU ,I WANNA KNOW IF IM INTERESTED IN WHAT I SEE -WHY WASTE BOTH PPLS TIME BEATING AROUND THE BUSH !!! YOU CAN ASK ME ANYTHING ,IM OPEN & ONLY WANT TO CHAT WITH OPEN PPL ~PRETTY SIMPLE HUH~ ..COMMINCATION IS EVERYTHING -WHY ADD DRAMA ,SHOW SOME RESPECT WE ARE NOT IN HIGH SCHOOL ! -SEEMS ALOT ON HERE JUST PLAYING GAMES & WASTING SOMEONE ELSE TIME - MY TIME IS VALVABLE TO ME, BE STRAIGHT UP, NO DRAMA, NO GAMES & NO BULLsh*t! IM HERE TO HAVE FUN , I WILL NOT TALK TO YOU IF YOUR BEATING AROUND THE BUSH ! IF YOUR MAMA DIDNT RAISE YOU NO BETTER THAN THAT

,GO SLAP HER AZZ! HEHE--WE AS KIDS & ALL KIDS DESERVE YOUR TIME AS MOMS & DADS -WHERE YOU THINK ALL THESE NO RESPECT IDIOTS COME FROM? CUS MOMS & DADS AINT TAKIN THE TIME TO TEACH THERE OWN CHILDREN RESPECT! HOPE I DIDNT PISS NOBODY OFF !

TOO FUNNY -I CANT BELIEVE I JUST WROTE ALL THAT --YUP IM GOOF -THX FOR READING!

Never Mind, I am not Speechless. Words to Live by From trickyazz

Let's revisit trickyazz. Upon further analysis, I have decided that I still think trickyazz isn't all that witty and cute as I mentioned in his chapter, but he does speak his truth. Buried between the all-caps print and the lack of punctuation, he speaks with wisdom and experience from which we can all learn. Let's look at his profile more carefully.

From the start, trickyazz shows that he knows the Golden Rule. *"-ever heard of 10 fold ??? -treat others the way u want tobe treated ???"* We can see he has been hurt, *"o when someone does it to u 10 times ,dont ask urself why ,its cus its same crap u done to someone else !!! go figure -ok sorry but if ur an idiot or bipolar or stuck on urself or dont reply back -- then leave me alone !!!!"*

All he is asking is that his date treats him well. He has been in contact with those who are insincere and he is rejecting this. We all would. In this next paragraph, trickyazz goes on to tell you who he is. He shows insightful self-awareness. He lists the things he loves to do, the qualities he possesses and how he views life:

love music that has meaning, mostly rock like (shinedown,seether,tool,fuel,staind ,nickelback) love country food ,im a goof mostly, im high on life, love to laugh, but know when tobe serious. im happy go lucky , dont need anyone trying change my roll. i know what i want in life & have goals, i love racing (i drive dirt track late model car), 4 wheeling, active, anything fun, watch dvd, going to river with my english bulldogs, spending time with kids, they deserve to have good fresh start on life when they get older, always been family man, love kids, im self employed for 20 years ,love my job & its flexible, not into the party scene, i like to go out to clubs play pool,foosball, drink very little, no drugs, dont mind if someone else does. i dont like mean or rude people. likes sex (freak in the bed) ,that thing has a shelf life & im going to use it! hehe! i never judge book by its cover.

Next, trickyazz is letting women know that he is not a user (he has his own money) and he is stating what he wants in a mate. He wants truth, he wants someone he can't live without, he wants to let someone shine. He doesn't want game-players, cynics, or pessimists. These are all qualities that have become important to him over time and experience. They are qualities most of us would agree are valuable.

i i got my own money, home, truck. i dont use people, i got my own, dont like fighting, fussing, drama. people can shine if no one is holding them back or controlling them, cant never could do nothing, not into playing games,,theres not much trust, truth, or respect for others now days . i can live with anyone, but i want the one i cant live with out!!! if you have been treated bad in your past by others -i didnt do it! your past is old history -leave it in the past & look forward to the future! why be unhappy one more day! get over it! so if ya wanna chat, look me up, drop me a line ,apply within

In one of his many updates, you can see trickyazz experiencing the same frustrations that many of us have experienced in online dating. We have all had dates who weren't exactly up front about themselves whether it be about looks, personality or whatever. He wants honesty and communication. He has had dates who pretended to be something they weren't. He is tired of it and expresses it:

UPDATE! HERE WE GO! THIS MIGHT NOT BE GOOD -BUT IM GOIN TO SAY IT ANYWAY -I HAVE NOTHING AGAINST DIFFERENT SIZE OR COLOR WOMEN -THERES SOMEONE OUT THERE FOR EVERYBODY , MAYBE IM PICKY ,BUT I DO KNOW WHAT IM ATRACTED TOO ~ I LIKE THICK OR CHUNKY CURVY WOMEN WITH BRAINS, WITH BOOBS -SORRY THATS JUST WHAT I LIKE -I DIDNT WANT TO PUT IT OUT HERE LIKE THIS -BUT IT SEEMS SOME PPL CANT READ OR DONT READ OR DONT UNDERSTAND WHAT THICK OR CHUNKY OR WITH BOOBS OR WITH BRAINS MEANS -SO GO ASK A FRIEND WHAT THEY THINK YOU ARE IF YOU DONT KNOW !!! -IM NOT TRYING TOBE A SMARTAZZZ HERE OR RUDE ,MEAN OR DEGRADE ANYBODY - BUT DAMMN WHERE DO THESE PEOPLE COME FROM, IF YOU CANT READ ,GO SLAP YO MAMA... HEHE! IM JUST SAYING WE ARE ALL DIFFERENT & WE HAVE THE RIGHT & A CHOICE OF WHAT WE LIKE ,AS WE ALL DO -BUT IF YOU GOIN TO HIDE THINGS -YOUR NOT READY TO EVEN MEET SOMEONE ! WE (WELL NOT SURE ABOUT EVERYBODY ELSE ,BUT SPEAKING FOR MYSELF.) IM HERE TRYING TO GET TO KNOW SOME NEW FRIENDS & GO FROM THERE !!! IF YOU CANT BE HONEST & SHOW SOME RESPECT ,KEEPING STEPIN !!! CUS I

DONT EVEN WANT TO CHAT WITH SOMEONE HIDING THINGS -ALL I HEAR MOST TIME -IS IM TRYING OR WORKING ON LOSING MORE WEIGHT ! GUESS WHAT -I DONT CARE - I LIKE BIGGER WOMEN 160 TO 300 DEPENDS ON BUTT,BOOBS,HEIGHT & HEALTH -I LIKE BIG BOOBS & CURVES -LIKE A WOMAN THAT EATS & IS HAPPY , DAMMN THE BOITCHING -IM A HAPPY GO LUCKY ,FUN PERSON ,& IM GOING TO STAY THAT WAY - IF YOU DONT FIT OR I DONT FIT WHAT WE BOTH WANT ,LET THE OTHER PERSON KNOW -I KNOW YOU TALK TO SOME PPL & WONDER WHY THEY SO DAMMN RUDE -I DO -BUT GUESS WHAT IM NOT HERE TO CHANGE YOU -IM HERE TO MEET SOMEONE THATS ON SAME PAGE -RESPECT & COMMINCATION IS MY BIGGEST THINGS -BE OPEN -BE YOURSELF -WHY PUT ON A FRONT -YOU ARE WHO YOU ARE -BUT IF I DO HAPPEN TO MEET YOU ,GUESS WHAT ITS NICE WHEN YOUR THE SAME PERSON OR LOOKS THE SAME AS IN PICTURES WHEN YOU MEET - PPL SEEM TO LIE ALOT !GO FIGURE !SO HAVE FEW DECENT PICTURES OF YOURSELF ~ WE ARE ALL DIFFERENT ,IN SHAPES, SIZES,

In his final update, trickyazz demonstrates that he understands the idea that sometimes people are just not a good fit for each other. He is fine with that as long as his dates are honest about where they stand and don't leave him hanging. This is a courtesy that everyone should expect and everyone should extend. Here is his dissatisfaction:

UPDATE! STOP WASTING MY TIME ! IF YOU NOT INTERESTED, SAY SO ,IF U DONT HAVE TIME SAY SO - LAST TIME I LOOKED ,THIS IS A ADULT SITE -WHICH MEANS SHOW SOME RESPECT TO OTHERS .. ~ JUST BE

NICE & SAY IM NOT INTERESTED AT THIS TIME ~ SAY WHAT U MEAN & MEAN WHAT U SAY GEEZ! IF YOU WANT TO PLAY A GAME ,IM NOT INTERESTED ! -IF SOMEONE ASK YOU SOMETHING & YOU DONT REPLY ,THAT MEANS YOUR HIDING SOMETHING -I MEAN IF IM GOIN TO CHAT WITH YOU ,I WANNA KNOW IF IM INTERESTED IN WHAT I SEE -WHY WASTE BOTH PPLS TIME BEATING AROUND THE BUSH !!! YOU CAN ASK ME ANYTHING ,IM OPEN & ONLY WANT TO CHAT WITH OPEN PPL ~PRETTY SIMPLE HUH~ ..COMMINCATION IS EVERYTHING -WHY ADD DRAMA ,SHOW SOME RESPECT WE ARE NOT IN HIGH SCHOOL ! -SEEMS ALOT ON HERE JUST PLAYING GAMES & WASTING SOMEONE ELSE TIME - MY TIME IS VALVABLE TO ME, BE STRAIGHT UP, NO DRAMA, NO GAMES & NO BULLsh*t! IM HERE TO HAVE FUN , I WILL NOT TALK TO YOU IF YOUR BEATING AROUND THE BUSH ! IF YOUR MAMA DIDNT RAISE YOU NO BETTER THAN THAT ,GO SLAP HER AZZ! HEHE--WE AS KIDS & ALL KIDS DESERVE YOUR TIME AS MOMS & DADS -WHERE YOU THINK ALL THESE NO RESPECT IDIOTS COME FROM? CUS MOMS & DADS AINT TAKIN THE TIME TO TEACH THERE OWN CHILDREN RESPECT! HOPE I DIDNT PISS NOBODY OFF !

While trickyazz has a very unique way of expressing himself, he is saying things that we have all felt. We all want someone to be honest, sincere and kind.

Trickyazz may just be my new hero.

The Angry Guy

Category 1: Those who are not ready to date.
Category 2: Those who fail to embrace their own reality.

People are funny. They take the time and make the effort (and it is an effort, I tell you) to sit down and write an online profile that represents who they are while being charming and open, and to find pictures that represent them at their best and most attractive. Then you weed through the vast array of emails and profiles to see who just might be a potential date. The idea is to attract someone to whom you would be attracted. You try to present yourself as someone people would want to be around. You want someone to see your profile and think, "Gee, that girl/guy would be a fun date!" or "I would like to meet her/him!" Or maybe that was just me. Maybe I was missing the point.

Here's the thing. I found many, many profiles from men who were obviously not trying to attract anyone. And if they thought they were, well, then they also fell into the category of "those who fail to embrace their own reality." By the way, I have never looked at women's profiles, but I am absolutely positive that this goes both ways. I merely use the men as examples because that is what I have seen. The problem with these men is that they are not over those who have done them wrong and done them wrong bad! They feel the need to vent, spew, and regurgitate all of the past women's grievous errors to anyone who will listen, and what better way to do it than in a profile designed to be viewed by women? I mean, it's like a gift...to have a website that allows you to tell women how ticked off you are at their mere existence and explain that "it's not me...it's all you women who are messed up."

The thing I find amusing is that I don't even think these men know they are doing this. I don't think they realize that they are making themselves completely unattractive to potential dates. Who wants to go out with someone who has this list of faults that you must avoid or become one of "those" women? I had a guy calling and texting once who was just weird. I told him I didn't think we were a match. I didn't criticize or list his faults. I just said we weren't a match. And do you know what he said to me? *"No wonder your husband left you."* I never met him, and I didn't really take it personally, but it is still not easy to hear something like that. I didn't blame him, but he was going to blame me for sure. He, by the way, will be the next exciting entry! Fetish Guy.

I digress. The point is that people who write profiles like these, and especially the ones who don't even realize they are doing it, are just not ready to be out there dating. No one wants someone who is angry. No one wants someone who doesn't like the opposite sex at the moment. No one wants the pressure of having to be perfect to avoid your previous issues. Obviously, online daters are all single (well, except the people who lie, but that's not what this entry is about) or we wouldn't be using a dating site. Chances are, most people have had one or several bad experiences with relationships. And none of us wants a liar, cheater, drama-filled nut case. Believe it or not, this goes WITHOUT saying! So I have some advice:

1. If you are still angry at your last (or any) significant other, do not write an online dating profile.

2. If you are still angry at your last (or any) significant other, do not ask your friends to set you up.

3. If you are still angry at your last (or any) significant other, do not date at all.

4. If you think you are past it and you do get online and find yourself listing all of the things that you do not want, then turn the computer off immediately.

5. If you think you are past it and find yourself online to date and write a nice profile, but are thinking of all the things you don't want with someone in your past in mind...try again later.

6. If you think you are past it, have some degree of optimism that there are decent people in the world, and then give it a go.

The following is the profile of the guy who is not ready to date that prompted this entry. I choose not to mention his glaring grammatical errors. I know he has some anger issues and probably can't deal with that right now. A few pages in, he instructs you to "climb back into the drama ditch where you crawled out of" if you can't handle the "truth." Sigh. I am thinking maybe he dug that ditch. And he probably wants to hide the bodies in it. Here it is (and by the way, his tag line really makes you want to keep reading, doesn't it? :

Quite Lying About Wanting a Nice Guy:

In fact most women on here need to just remove every statement about wanting to find someone respectable...

someone faithful... someone who is nice... someone who will treat them well.... totally from there profile... because most every woman on here who says that is truly lying....

I have made an attempt to talk to more than one lady on here.... and i am respectable... and i don't talk rude to anyone.... but it is rare for anyone to respond to my letters..... and the ones who respond... talk for once or twice... then go back to the drama they say they dont want...

Why are women so afraid to actually give someone a chance who is worth anything.... why do women only go for someone who will never treat them right.... is drama so much a part of there lives that they cant live without it???

if drama is all you want.... im not what you are looking for....

someone who cheats on you???? thats not me...

someone who will take advantage of you.... again... not me...

someone who will treat you like crap.... find someone else.... im not that way...

I have a job and work hard at it.... I pay my bills... so i guess since im not going to be living off of you... im not good enough...

Family is important to me.... in fact i take care of my mother... so if this is unappealing to you.... find someone else who hates his family....

I know i look good.... and i take care of myself.... so if you want a slob who looks like crap every day.... move on....

I just got a great set of wheels that i am proud of.... so if you want to ride around in a junker.... again... move on....

I am an intelligent free thinking person.... who can carry on a great conversation... so if you want a brain dead moron.... theres plenty of them out there....

Im active... i enjoy going out and doing things.... Skydiving... Cave exploration... traveling... so if you want a lazy piece of crap.... your looking in the wrong place....

I know how to listen.... on top of good conversations.... and if i am with someone... there opinion truly matters to me.... so if you want someone who would rather shut you up... plenty of abusive bad boys out there..... get over it... you will never change them or "save" them...

And why have people tried to hook me up with people who are fat and lazy????? Im in shape.... im healthy... im active.... if your not going to be able to keep up.... then your not the person for me.... im not going to stop being active because you are out of shape... Its not my fault that you cant keep up....

and why should i even want to be with someone who is way above my weight class????? I dont care if you have a "great" personality..... if thats all your bringing to the table... your a few cards short.....

im offering the great personality... good looks.... active life.... faithfulness... Romance... respect.... and true happiness....

If you cant offer the same.... how would i ever be happy??? i would be nothing but your slave then....

This is a true to life poem i wrote.... that proves how women cry about what they want.... and only settle for everything they complain about....

You dream of someone who is a gentleman.

You settle for someone who is a total caveman.

You dream of someone who will listen.

You settle for someone who never hears anything you say.

You dream of someone who truly cares about your dreams.

You settle for someone who who always puts you last.

You dream of someone who will fill your life with passion.

You settle for someone who only breaks your heart.

You dream of someone who gladly makes you happy.

You settle for someone who laughs at you when you are sad.

You dream of someone who will comfort you when are scared.

You settle for someone who thinks you never deserve comfort.

You dream of someone who will help you with the housework.

You settle for someone who only yells when you are not working like his slave.

You dream of someone who will gladly give you his time.

You settle for someone who is around you when he feels you might deserve his time.

You dream of someone who shares his whole heart with you.

You settle for someone who does not have emotions.

You dream of someone who will trust you when you are apart from him.

You settle for someone who constantly accuses you of cheating.

You dream of someone who will defend you with his life.

You settle for someone who always starts fights with everyone who just looks at you.

If you have children.

You dream of someone who will accept your children and care for them as his own.

You settle for someone who thinks your kids are nothing more than a burden.

First DateI dont care if you think im an a$$... no one cared when i was nothing but respectable.... guess its time for me to be truly blunt....

if you cant handle the truth.... you need to just climb back into the drama ditch where you crawled out of.... im looking for true happiness....

I will have no problem coming up with a good first date. Even if it is simple. It will be memorable.

For a date can be as simple as a walk in a park. To exciting as jumping out of an airplane.

There is nothing "normal" of what i can create.

Fetish Guy AKA Panty Hose Guy

Category 1: Just plain weird.

Category 2: I love you, but I've never met you.

Category 3: Those who are so busy telling you how great they are that they don't notice how great you are.

Category 4: Too much too fast.

Dating Tips:

1. If someone is tooting his own horn, it's probably because no one else is tooting it.

I still have trouble with this one, and I have had at least a couple of years to process it. I think that in general, a guy who has to tell you how great he is probably isn't. It's kind of like people who tell you how Christian they are. Actions speak louder, right?

Fetish Guy was from Ohio, if I remember correctly. This was one of those learning experiences. I learned that if someone lives that far away, no thanks. I learned that if someone has to toot his own horn, it's probably because no one else is tooting it. I learned that if someone sets expectations on you before you've even met, run far, far away.

BIG RED FLAG

The first phone call consisted of his long dissertation on what a great date he can plan. He flew one girl to Disney World (she had no kids by the way, he just loved theme parks). He would fly you, wine you and dine you. Even at this earlier stage of my dating experience, I thought this guy had a too much too fast issue. I really don't want to meet someone for the first time when he has paid for a flight, a hotel room, and a theme park visit. That is waaaaaay too much pressure and his lofty expectations made him feel validated by his extravagant spending.

He also wanted details on my divorce. That is not a first conversation conversation. I gave him a very fluffy, benign, no-details kind of story. He wasn't totally satisfied, but too bad. I hate it when people pressure you to talk about personal things. That is an evolution, not an expectation. Oddly, this happens pretty frequently in dating life. Some people use it as a test. Are you open? Are you willing to tell your secrets? Will you do what I ask you to do? This last trait (controlling) hits his nail on the head and becomes foreshadowing. If only I had seen it…

BIG RED FLAG

At that point he launched into questions. Do you like to call and text? I like to know the person I'm with is thinking of me, he said. I like little notes and texts throughout the day, he said. Okay, I thought. That's fine. Who doesn't like to be thought of, right?

A little more conversation, nothing too unusual. And then...

BIG RED FLAG

"Do you wear pantyhose?"
"What?"
"Do you wear pantyhose. I love women who wear pantyhose."
"Uh, well, I live in Florida, and it's, you know, 100 degrees half the time, so not really."
"Would you if I wanted you to? Wouldn't you do that for someone who cared about you?"
"I don't even own a pair, and I detest it." (And I'm thinking, you don't know me well enough to care about me.)
"But wouldn't you want to make your man happy?"

Now let me interject here. "Your man?" This is still the first conversation. "Your man?" Seriously. And do you notice the test?
He went on.

"Wouldn't you do something for your man even if you didn't really like it...just to make him happy?"
"Well, yes, but why would you ask me to do that if you knew I hated it? And I would never ask someone to do something they hated."

Deal Breaker

"Because you have to be willing to give in a relationship..."

On and on he went. And once again, I ask, "in a relationship?" Too much too fast.

The next week he started to call on a pretty regular basis and send little texts throughout the day. I'm not sure what he did for a living because after the first call, I didn't really care; but he drove a lot during the day and would call between stops. I answered when I could, but I spend a good bit of the day on the phone at work and many times I couldn't. He would leave little messages...just thinking about you, etc. It was easier to respond to his texts, but even those got to be so frequent that I didn't always answer each one. My fault in the situation was that I didn't take my own advice and use my handy exit line sooner. As the week passed, he started to get annoyed when I didn't answer immediately. He left messages that became more and more snide.

"Guess you are busy, call me back."
"Too busy for me?"
"What are you doing?"
"Miss me?"
"I guess you can't make time for me in your busy day."

Again, seriously?

Finally, after a little more than a week, I sent him a text after one of his many texts that day and I said the following:

"I really think this is a little bit too much. We are not in a relationship, and I think you are expecting too much too fast. I don't think this is going to work out."

His response:
"Well, no wonder your husband left you."

I guess I should have told him we weren't a good fit instead. Live and learn.

And that was that.

No wonder he was single.

Things I Don't Get

I had been back in the dating pool for about five years. After all of this time filled with (mostly) blog-worthy dates, there were things I understood and things I didn't. There were people who showed a little kindness and people who shocked the heck out of me. There were people who were paralyzed by their past experiences and people who dated in such a rapid-fire manner that I don't think they knew what they wanted or how to get it.

Let's start with something that I get. I get that at my age, most potential dates have been through some things in life. I don't know anyone who has managed to escape some kind of pain. Most have been through divorce. And I think that from divorce (anything painful, really) comes fear. Fear enters the equation in several ways. You fear being hurt. You fear being alone. Most of all you fear that you will not see things clearly. You doubt your ability to trust yourself to see who people really are, and you distrust your ability to make the hard choices when you do see them clearly. For myself, I had a lot of fear. I know that no divorce is easy...there is no such thing as a "good" divorce. In my experience, I found out that during the whole of my marriage I did not know the truth, even for a moment. So I had fear about seeing things clearly, knowing who someone is, and trying not to question everything in my own mind. I get fear.

That leads me to something I don't get. I don't get why people, men and women, stay in situations when they do see things clearly and they know it is wrong. This happens on a shockingly regular basis. It is true for men and for women. I have seen friends who are consistently treated badly, manipulated, used, criticized, and on and on. My lack of understanding comes when they realize they are being treated this way, and for some reason, which is completely foreign to me, keep beating their heads against the wall of sanity.

I had a conversation with a friend the other day who lamented the fact that he was still attracted to someone who was clearly bad for him. She used him to fill the gaps when she was alone; she wanted him around when she wanted him. He wondered why he was still attracted to her. "She's a nut-job," he said. "I shouldn't be attracted to her." He had the self-awareness required to see his situation clearly, but where was the fortitude?

It is hard to be alone. I get that. But it is not okay to be with someone who treats you badly (just plain jerks), makes you feel less (insecure), wants you only when it's convenient for them (power-trip/manipulator) or strings you and five other suckers along (control freak/attention seeker). I have been on the receiving end of most of these types of people through the years, but only until I see the game. I am the queen of the quick exit when I see any of these **BIG RED FLAGS**. They are there for a reason, and we should use them!

Again. Big Red Flags are there for a reason. Use them!

I have said many times that I would rather be alone for the rest of my life than be with the wrong person. Repeat after me:

I would rather be alone for the rest of my life than be with the wrong person.

Next, I get anger. Let me tell you, when you find out that a third of your life was a lie, it will definitely tick you off. There may even be a period of hating everyone of the opposite sex on principle. I think I managed to avoid this one because I feel pretty sure there aren't many as extreme as that one. If I'm wrong, well, the world is a sad, sad place. My anger was there, just very specifically aimed. I know a lot of people who have spewed anger at a general gender. I am sure a period of anger is probably even healthy, as long as it is LIMITED.

I don't get it when people are still in the angry phase and think they are ready to date. If an angry person is dating online, it is nearly impossible to hide the anger in what they have to say on their profiles. There is usually a very specific list of things they do not want: liars, cheaters, druggies. Those are obvious. Sometimes the criteria are more subtly coded. It comes disguised in a "what I want" sentence, but really it's a "what I don't want" sentence. I want an "independent" woman means I don't want someone who is after my money. I want someone who is "active" means no overweight people need apply.

There may also be a list of things they hate. I hate drama. I hate psychos. I hate whiners. The thing I want to say to these men (I am sure women do it, too; I just haven't read women's profiles) is this: THESE THINGS GO WITHOUT SAYING!! No one likes these things. And by listing them you are telling the world exactly what has happened to you in your last relationship(s). Ultimately, it makes you look like a whiner and someone who isn't over your last relationship. This is not the way to attract people to you.

I would rather be alone for the rest of my life than be with the wrong person.

I also get that there are times when you don't know exactly what you want or don't want, and so you want to date around. I think this is pretty healthy. I think sometimes we get an idea in our heads of what we want and that may limit who we would meet. I have seen many people end up dating someone who wasn't the idea of their "type." I think getting stuck on a type could potentially lock out someone great that you never would have noticed.

The thing I don't get is when you want to date around and you don't make that clear to your dates. It is only fair to let people know where you stand. When you know your date is more interested in you than you are in them, it is not fair not to let them know where you are in your dating mind. I have also been on the receiving end of this. Usually people are fine with the truth, even if feelings get a bit hurt. The truth always hurts less than making someone wonder or allowing them to believe something that isn't true. And if someone is in a different place from you, do them the courtesy of allowing them to decide based on what really is, not what you have let them think it is.

After all, I would rather be alone for the rest of my life than be with the wrong person.

I get wanting to find someone. Most people don't want to be alone and are searching to find "The One." I have certainly been on more dates than I thought I would ever go on.

I don't get the whole too much too fast syndrome. I have experienced many of these types. The ones who get attached when you have never met. Sometimes it's almost all by text; other times, calls and texts. They start talking immediately about the future and making plans. One guy kept saying "I'm all in." The fact that I wouldn't say that after two phone conversations really annoyed him. As one friend likes to tell me, I know you are great, but a total stranger doesn't know you well enough to know that.

They fall into two of the blog categories: One: I love you but I've never met you, and Two: I just want to get married and you will do. Either of these ideas makes you feel kind of sick. After having a large part of my life turn out to be a lie, I take some time to get to know someone. I have to. And I sometimes even say to these kinds of men, "I could be a nut; you have no idea after five minutes." And who wants to be the "you will do" kind of girlfriend? Don't you want to be liked for who you actually are on the inside?

Again, I would rather be alone for the rest of my life than be with the wrong person.

Now don't misunderstand--I would rather not be alone. I have a good life, good kids and a good job. I would still like someone to share it with; but I have been through enough pain, and I will not do that again. I certainly don't expect perfection; I just want, you know, the little things like honor, character, humor, and love. Easy peasy, right? Someone recently asked me what the key to my parents' 42-year marriage was. The answer came immediately. They put each other first.

Easy Peasy.

The Woe is Me Guy

Category 1: Poor pitiful me.
Category 2: Those who are not ready to date.

Of all the categories of dates or profiles I have come upon, the most horrible, awful, sad, frustrating and annoying one is the Woe is Me Guy. This attitude, oddly, has been a running theme in my life. Oddly, because I don't think I am a woe-is-me type girl...or if I am my self-awareness is lower than I thought. I have, however, attracted two woe-is-me type guys. One I dated for four years; the other I was married to for 10. I am big on self-awareness, so I'm sure that says something about me...a story for another day.

With these types, I find that you end up spending every ounce of energy trying to make these people feel better about themselves....better about who they are, what they do, how they act...better about how you feel about them, how much you want them. It's exhausting. And if you don't fulfill this need, then somehow it is your fault that they are woe is me. So, finding happiness and joy with someone who is hell-bent on feeling sorry for himself is a no-win situation.

Helpful Hints AKA BIG RED FLAGS

If you find you are with someone who has said any, and I mean any, of the following, run Forrest, run:

1. Well, I am leaving you a voicemail, so either you are busy or avoiding my calls. [This one is designed to make you feel guilt whether you have done something wrong or not. Run.]

2. Your actions speak that you are not as into me as I am into you. I don't have time or room for that in my life. [Run. You will probably never be able to feed that kind of need.]

3. I just don't think I am good enough for you (or, in the reverse, you are too good for me). [This one is designed to elicit a speech from you touting the enormous...and it better be enormous... list of stellar attributes that you love about him/her. And then you must spend time convincing him/her that it is, in fact, true. Run. You will be making lists until the end of time.]

4. I think you like so-and-so better than you like me. [The best answer to this is a simple, "yes." Less work than running and definitely less work than the convincing game this manipulator is trying to make you play.]

5. You never respond to my texts; I guess you aren't thinking about me during your day. [Run like hell. You will never convince this person that you might actually be BUSY, even though you might be busy and thinking of him/her and just can't take time to tell him/her. You

know, working, taking care of kids, etc. This is called the case of the self-absorbed.]

I have a brief yet shining example of a Woe is Me Guy whose profile is below. This guy has a graduate degree and is nice looking. It is astounding that he thinks that whining and lamenting is a way to attract a woman. Maybe he just needs a forum to whine. There has to be a better place to do that than Match.com. At any rate, he winked at me, and I read it and hit delete. I have learned my lesson about the "poor me" syndrome. It's a real downer:

LostSoul
Nice guy who always finishes last! Tired of treating women like gold and having them walk all over me! Ready to have someone treat me like I treat them. Tired of meeting the "damaged" ones! Maybe one day I will meet the right one but I doubt it!

He should add the line: Sigh. Woe is me.
Or maybe it works better implied.

The "Cheating" Guy

Category 1: Those who are not ready to date.
Category 2: Those who fail to embrace their own reality.

Dating Tips:

   1. Lunch-hour dates are a great idea. Getting back to work limits the date and you never feel stuck.

Divorce is hard. It is hard to decide to do. It is hard to face. It is hard to tell your friends you are doing it. There are feelings of embarrassment that you couldn't make it work. There is fear of what people will think. Will they think it was me? Will they suspect things that happened or, even worse, things that didn't happen? It is not fun. Ever. But when it happens, like it or not, you've just got to man up and face the facts.

This guy **seemed normal...**

He was divorced, educated, nice, former military, and had a couple of kids. On the phone, he seemed very normal (very, because there are degrees of normal. You would think normal is an absolute, wouldn't you...but it's not!). He had some humor, spoke and had interesting stories.

We met at Starbucks for coffee during my lunch hour. As an aside, this is a great first date. There is a predetermined time limit. It is a public place and no financial investment. And most are small enough that every seat is near the exit. Even better, if you eat outside, all you have to do is get in your car. Perfect!

Back to "Cheating" Guy. The quotation marks become relevant very soon. He beat me to Starbucks and had a table. He said, *"If you don't mind, I'd like to sit facing the window. I ...I ah...have some PTSD. You know, from the military. I have to be able to see people coming and going."*

Okay. I understand a thing or two about PTSD. And I wouldn't think as much about that with a military guy. But first thing out of his mouth? That is a "let's ease into it" conversation. So, a little too much information right off the bat, but I'm not too worried about it.

Once he started talking....

BIG RED FLAG AFTER BIG RED FLAG

This guy was not ready to man up.

"My wife and I, I mean my ex-wife..."
"I really hate that I don't get to see my kids that much." He had them half the time.
"You are my first date since the divorce."

Seriously? No kidding. So not ready. This is an interesting situation because everyone has to have a first date after the divorce. The trick is to try and find dates in similar places. Someone who is ready for something more serious should probably not have to break in a newbie. Way different places.

Back to the story. I am not knocking any of his sentiments. We have all been there. It is hard for some people to change terminology from wife to ex-wife or husband to ex-husband. Me...not so much. But I can see a transitional period. It is very difficult to have time where your kids are away from you. I have mine twenty-six days a month and it still was an adjustment. And we all have to start somewhere. As I said, there will have to be a first date after the divorce.

When you say something like what follows, however, you are not ready for the first date after the divorce. Here it is. Brace yourself:

"Sitting here with you having coffee, I feel like I am cheating on my wife."

I wanted to get up and leave right there and say, "Dude, you are prematurely dating." But I didn't. I tried to be kind and understand his feelings. I tried to keep my shock on the inside where it belonged rather than let it show on my always-readable face.

Do I really need to say more? I don't think he had failed to embrace his own reality, I think he was denying his own reality. And if you have been through the whole process of the divorce and you are still saying things like that, you are NOT READY TO DATE.

Shockingly, I never heard from him again. Can you believe it?

The All In Guy

Category 1: The too much too fast syndrome.
Category 2: I love you but I've never met you.
Category 3: I want to get married and you will do.

All In Guy had a very nice profile. He didn't seem angry, bitter, holding on to his last relationship...no apparent red flags. He was educated, had a job and wrote an upbeat little profile. So when he wrote a note, I responded. He moved to a phone call that same day. I always appreciate that because you get a feel for a person so much better over the phone as a general rule.

The phone call was nice. Good old Alabama boy. Loved the South, sports, Alabama football. A bit of a sports fanatic, but a guy's guy. We talked easily and had a good, funny dynamic off the bat. And then I asked him how many online dates he'd had so far...

BIG RED FLAG

"You are the first."

The dreaded words...you are the first. Ugh! Still, I gave him the benefit of the doubt. He went on to say that he had dated someone since his divorce, just not from meeting online. I wasn't his first date...that made it okay. Or so I thought.

The phone conversation continued. He talked about wanting to get a place on the water about forty-five minutes from where I live.

BIG RED FLAG

"Are you committed to Pensacola, or are you willing to move?"

This question can be legitimate, but the first conversation is a bit early for this talk. How about are you committed to having coffee? The moving point could be moot after half a cup. I still didn't think that was a huge deal. Some people like to set their boundaries right off the bat. Not a deal breaker at this point. And then...

BIG RED FLAG

"I lost the boat in the divorce," he said. "But I will get another one when I move to the water."

Ok, here's the thing...if you bring up what you "lost in the divorce" in the first conversation with a girl...it sends so many wrong messages. First, you are bitter. I understand the feeling, but if you are not past it enough not to feel compelled to share it with a total stranger, maybe not ready to date. Second, you are still angry. Once again, not ready to date.

Conversation continued.

He said he had been online for about two weeks. He had looked at profile after profile and decided that mine was the one he liked. Now that is flattering. Who wouldn't enjoy that statement? Right? And then he said, *"Now that we have talked, and we get along, I want to meet you. I am a one-at-a-time kind of guy and I'm not looking at anyone else's profile."*

Okay, that is a bit much. I decided he was just an inexperienced online dater. Who commits to someone after one phone conversation? To be honest, I thought he was joking. He wanted to meet as soon as possible. That weekend I had a full schedule. He kept trying to talk me into squeezing him in or inviting him to things I had planned. One thing I don't do is invite a total stranger to events with my friends. It's just odd. And pressure.

I decided I could meet him for a drink early that Friday before dinner with friends. We had talked earlier in the day, and he called on the way. He kept talking about wanting to kiss me. Once again, a little much, sight unseen. I chalked it up to inexperience again. I got to the bar (can you guess?...on the water, outdoor deck) first...told him where I was sitting and that I was wearing a green dress. And nothing. He was five minutes out. Five minutes later, nothing. Then 10 minutes. Nothing. I looked at my phone and he had called, but I didn't hear it. So I called. No answer. I called again. No answer.

Okay. The mind reels at this point. Did he see me and run the other direction? Did I miss him coming in? Did he get the wrong place? And back to did he see me and flee? Finally he called back. He said that he went in the bar and I wasn't there. I described where I was sitting and he said there was no one there. At this point I do not believe anything he says. He said he asked the bartender if there was a girl in a green dress and she said there wasn't. I could not have missed all that. So I don't believe him.

By this time I am back home, and he says, *"Well, you will just have to meet me at my kids' baseball practice and we can make out there."*

Seriously. He said that. And baseball was 45 minutes from my house. And I don't know this guy. And I don't trust him at all. Not going to happen. I still can't figure out how the bar thing went wrong. He asks me to send a pic of the green dress so that I can prove I was there. I did.

"You are beautiful," he said. Yeah, right.

"I don't know what to say to that," I said.

"Say forever," he responded.

Yeah right. He's either got a flare for the dramatic, or he is waaaaay too much too fast.

And then he continued to try to talk me into meeting him. Nope.

He wanted to try for Sunday. I said we'll see.

Friday night I was at dinner with a few friends and I got a text from him. *"How's the date going?"*

"What?'

"Yeah right," he says.

That was beyond it for me. I told him I had plans. He assumed it was a date. Frankly, if it was a date (it wasn't) I was entitled. I had never met this guy. Holy Cow!

I decided that was that. He texted the next day, and I said I didn't think I wanted to meet. He was not happy, but I didn't hear from him the rest of the weekend. Several days later, I got a text. He "accidentally" wrote to me thinking it was his brother. Okay. Then he launched into this: One minute we were talking about forever, and the next you were breaking my heart.

I tried to explain that I was never talking about forever. And then:

"You are either all in or you are all out," he said. *"Which is it?"*

"All out." This came as a surprise to him. Almost nothing surprises me anymore...but this guy did.

Interestingly, had I recognized all of the clues in this story, I would have seen things more clearly much sooner. If someone you have never met asks you if you are willing to move, he is too much too fast. If someone insists that you meet when you have told him that your weekend is full, then he is trying to control your time. If someone you have never met tries to make you feel awkward because he assumes you lied about your time or that you are not entitled to be on a date with someone else, he is insecure and manipulative. All of these hints in our conversations were Big Red Flags into the dynamic of his relationships.

And they were there for a reason.

The Walmart Parking Lot Guy

Category 1: Those who kind of freak you out.

So he **seemed normal,** checked off the list of acceptable criteria...except for one thing...he was 6'6". I love a tall guy, as I have mentioned before, but 6'6" is oddly tall. I didn't fully comprehend the oddity until I came face-to-face, or should I say face-to-rib cage?

We met at the beach on a warm and not-a-cloud-in-the-sky kind of day. It was even kind of sweet that he wanted to meet to take a walk on the beach. I can't tell you how many people actually state the desire for a beach walk in profiles, but never once had I been invited for such a date until Mr. Tall. We met at the beach-ball-shaped water tower on Pensacola Beach. After making our initial small talk, we started to walk. It didn't take me long to realize that his long, lanky stroll amounted to a trot for me to keep up. I don't know how long I thought we would go, but we walked...and walked...and walked some more.

Now, I don't know if it is apparent, but I have a competitive streak. I was NOT going to ask him to slow down, nor was I going to huff and puff and let him see the effort it was taking for me to keep up. It became a personal mission to look cool and collected while trotting.

Finally, after what I think is about a mile and a half, we got to Peg Leg Pete's, a beach restaurant, can you guess? With an outdoor deck and view of the water. Thank goodness he wanted to get a beer and eat! Rest. Maybe I will make it back!

Dinner was good. Conversation flowed. Normal, normal, normal! Good news.

And then...the dreaded walk back. I blame the beer and food, but before even a third of the way back, I had to swallow my pride and say, "Hey...you take seriously big steps....you think we can slow down a bit?"

"Sure! Need a break?"

This was the excuse he must have needed to try a kiss. This part cracked me up...not the kiss itself, it was fine. But the maneuvering required for him to kiss someone a foot shorter. Instead of bending to reach, he stood with his feet a good yard or more apart so he didn't have to bend down. I don't know why I found that so funny, but it cracked me up! So he kissed me standing in the biggest ballet Second Position I had ever seen.

Every five minutes or so on the way back, he took time to let me rest and give me a kiss. He seemed nice, and I was enjoying the date (minus the trotting), so why not? The only thing was, with each progressive break, he became a little more aggressive. As we got closer, I tried to start emphasizing that I had to go relieve the babysitter. It was dark, on the beach and with few other people around. I wasn't worried, but safety, safety, safety.

When we finally made it back to our cars, he started talking about getting together again. Okay, I thought. This was a decent first date. Why not?

"Let's meet tomorrow night," he said. *"I want to see you tomorrow."*

I couldn't make such spur of the moment plans at that time because my kids were younger and I needed a sitter. I told him I would see what I could work out.

"Even if it's just for a little while," he said. *"We can meet at the Walmart parking lot down the road there to make out."*

Long – really, really long and uncomfortable pause – to process this tidbit.

Really? He didn't just ask me out to the Walmart parking lot. How many levels of wrong is that? I rate a Walmart parking lot? Is he destitute and can't afford even a McDonald's? I'm not one of those who requires a lot. I am usually thrilled with not being asked to Sweeten the Deal on a date. Really. I am pretty easy to please. But the Walmart parking lot? If I had only known at that time that I would eventually write this book,

I could have thought of it as a gift.

The Parking Lot Guy
AKA Mr. Meow

Category 1: Those who do not learn from others' mistakes.

Category 2: Those who do not take "no" for an answer.

As usual, Parking Lot Guy **seemed normal**. He was tall. Yea! He had an education and a job. Nice! He had a son he adored. **SEEMED** like a nice, normal guy. I think we can all agree at this point that "seem" is a four-letter word in my life. Most people are not what they seem. The trick is to see how long they can keep "normal" up. So I often wonder, are some people better projecting normal than others or am I just getting better at discerning the nutcases? It is probably a combination of both.

Sorry--tangent.

So I had lunch with Parking Lot Guy. We went to a sports bar, had a nice lunch and good conversation. He was a little bit shy, but that was fine because I don't have a problem filling the silence as long as there is some participation from the guy. I do actually want to get to know people, and I can't do that by being the only one talking.

BIG RED FLAG

An aside that becomes relevant later...during lunch, I kept hearing this noise coming from his direction. It was like something in the back of his throat. Hard to describe in words, but it was a little tone, almost a quick hum, from high to low. It was purr-like or a sort of meow. This was perplexing. Did he know he was doing it? Was it a nervous habit? Was I imagining it? My mind reeled. Internal dialog ran amok. At times I couldn't focus on the conversation because I was anxiously awaiting the next meow to see if it was all in my mind or if he was aware he was doing it. Every time it occurred, I analyzed his face to see if he had a reaction...a glimmer of awareness. How could he not look even slightly self-conscious since I was exceedingly conscious. Such a mystery.

Another aside. If there is something like a meow distracting you from focusing on the actual date, NOT A GOOD SIGN.

After lunch we walked down the street to the park at the pier. Beautiful day. Nice walk. We sat on the benches at the pier and looked at the water. He was shy and sweet. He held my hand...very sweet...and didn't try to get fresh with me. And as hard as I tried, I didn't hear the meow. Good news.

The next day, he invited me to drive to Alabama and said he would show me around his area. Since I didn't have the kids that weekend, it was an easy plan. We met at the outlet mall, had a little lunch at Panera and then got in his car to see the sights. He had a convertible, so this was a perfect day for a drive....a long, long, endless drive. Apparently there was no destination. He drove me by some work he had engineered. He drove me through downtown. He drove me down rural roads.

He stopped for gas and chewing gum at a convenience store in the middle of nowhere. And he drove some more. I hadn't thought to ask, but I assumed we would stop at some sight to see somewhere and see a sight. Not to be. Note to self: Always know the plan ahead of time.

One of the things we had discussed on our date the day before was our experience with first dates. I relayed the Walmart parking lot story to him and he laughed and laughed. So you can imagine my surprise when after three hours...let me say it again...three hours of driving, he pulled into a parking lot. It was not Walmart, so let's just stop to give him a little ovation just for that. It was some industrial area near the interstate.

"Is this ok?" he asked.

"What? What are we doing?"

He kind of giggled.

I was thinking, really? He is not. He is not pulling into a parking lot. Well, hell.

So he said, *"I have been wanting to do this all day."*

Well, crap.

He leaned in for a kiss. Short and sweet. So, okay, not that bad. But then he curled up and put his head on my shoulder. Did I mention he was 6'3"? He had to scoot way down in his seat to even accomplish the head on my shoulder position. I don't know why I feel this way, but a big, grown man slinking down to put his head on a woman's shoulder is kind of weird. I felt like I should pat him on the back and tell him everything would be okay. It was little-boyish, I guess.

Alas, the shoulder position didn't last long. He moved back in for the kiss. And there it was...the meow. Now, considering that I was a little bit miffed by the whole parking lot thing after I had told him the error of Walmart Parking Lot

Guy's ways, and the fact that I had a destinationless date, I would have stopped him sooner, but the fact that he was meowing was just, well, fascinating. So I let him kiss me a little longer than was comfortable (well, none was comfortable) while I tried to figure it out. I couldn't. The whole time he kissed, he meowed in the back of his throat. I have to say, hands down, weirdest kiss I have ever had. It was kind of a whimper meow. I still can't figure it out.

I finally had to say that I needed to get home as my kids were coming back soon. I didn't ask about the meowing. I wish I had. It's a question that comes to me every now and then. An unsolved mystery. I did have the nerve to say, "I can't believe you took me to a parking lot." He laughed at my "joke." I guess it's better for him that he thought it was a joke.

He spared his own feelings.

The Dysautonomia Guy

Category 1: The ones that kind of freak you out.

Dating Tips:

1. You are allowed to be freaked out by the ones who exhibit freaky behavior.

This guy wrote me a nice note. Upon looking at his profile, he seemed to meet all of the basic requirements. He was the right age, picture looked normal (although knowing what I now know, why would I even write that sentence...). He was educated, had a job, could put together a sentence. Okay, so I will reply. In writing back and forth, he was funny. I like funny. And smart. I like smart. So off to a good start.

So we moved to phone calls. It is always funny when you talk to someone for the first time on the phone after writing to each other. There are times when the voice just does not match the idea in your head. So when he called....Holy Southern Accent, dude! I think there are Southern accents, and there are redneck accents. He lacked the grammatical errors of the stereotypical redneck accent, but phew! He had a DRAWL. He even said, *"I know my accent is probably a surprise to you. I get that a lot."* Gross understatement. But...moving on!

We talked on the phone a lot. He called every night. He seemed really interested, and in talking, despite the ACCENT, he was well-educated and knowledgeable. And then he said, *"So your ex-husband is a lawyer."*

BIG RED FLAG

And the reason it was a big red flag was because I hadn't mentioned my ex-husband. I learned early in the dating experience that telling someone too much about the bad things can cause regrets later. It is a story I don't tell easily. So imagine the flash of panic that he knew anything I hadn't told him. Was he playing a game? Did he know "he who shall remain nameless"? What did he know? How did he know? So I asked.

I had told him my maiden name and, because we had both grown up in Pensacola, we had talked about where we went to high school and tried to decide if we had any mutual friends. From those two pieces of information, he did research on the computer and knew where I went to college. He found my marriage license and, therefore, my married name. He Googled me and found my place of employment. He Googled my ex-husband and knew where he went to school, when we were divorced, that he worked for my father before and knew where he was working then.

I can't describe the awful tingle of creepiness that crawled up my spine. I had a stalker situation for two years in college, and I was sure that despite my over-sensitivity to that kind of leering into my life, this was still creepy. When he sensed that this wasn't a funny little thing he had just revealed, he said, *"Aren't you doing the same thing?"*

He said I should be doing the same thing. He said to go do it and he would expect it. So, of course, I did. And by the way, I can explain away all of the lawsuits, he said. He did some real estate business, and there are always lawsuits going on about something. I do think that can be true, but the sheer length of the list under his name in the Clerk of the Court website was disturbing.

As you can imagine, my comfort level plummeted.

The other thing weighing on my mind was that during all of our talks, he had revealed that he had an illness. He had something called dysautonomia, and had sought me out because my profile showed my job as a representative for Social Security disability claimants. He thought I was perfect and a "gift from God" because I would understand his situation and be empathetic. He said mostly he was fine, but he had some issues.

I understood his situation alright. I had a client with this same thing. It is horrible. It causes all of the systems in your body that control autonomic function to fail or go awry. The symptoms include fainting, extremely low blood pressure, inappropriate feelings of intense heat or cold, breathing problems, and extreme nausea. It is horrible.

He told me about one time when his mother came to check on him and his blood pressure was so low that she couldn't find a pulse and thought he was dead. We were supposed to meet once and he cancelled because he was too sick. We never did meet. I realized his was a bad case even for the diagnosis.

This kind of information does all kinds of things to your conscience. I was feeling freaked out already by the amount of research he had done. But I didn't know what to think of the fact that he had sought me out because of my job. My job is hard. It is emotionally draining. Back then, I was still working on keeping some emotional distance at work so it didn't get to me every night when I tried to sleep. I had clients who would tell me that if I didn't win their case, they wouldn't have a place to live or food to eat. I didn't want his illness to factor into my thoughts, but I was also just coming off of a time filled with my son's diagnosis of epilepsy and a solid year of regular seizures. I wanted an area of my life to feel lighter and easier and fun.

The way he described how he decided to write to me made me feel like he just wanted me to take care of him. I knew you would understand, he said. I knew you wouldn't be afraid. I knew you would be there. Is that fair? Is it fair to use the internet to find someone to take care of you? In my mind, I wanted to find someone who could take care of me as much as I of them. Was it heartless of me to think such thoughts?

And there was the creepy feeling of being researched. I couldn't get past that. It was a lot spinning in my head. I would never have left a spouse that came down with an illness. When I love someone I love them all the way. But how do you feel about starting something with someone who chose you as a nurse maid. Ugh!!!

In the end I wrote him a note that I just thought we were not a good fit. He didn't take it well. On dating sites, you can see who is viewing your profile. He relentlessly viewed my profile for years. I am not kidding. It was years. And it was often. He continued calling for a long time and even continued to "wink" at my profile years later. This caused unceasing little twinges of that creepy feeling as well as the twinges of the conscience.

The conscience was relieved to a degree as time went on because the creepy, stalking factor began to outweigh it.

The Rude Dude

Category 1: Those who leave your mouth agape with their rudeness.
Category 2: Too much too fast.
Category 3: Master of the backhanded compliment.

I don't really even remember how I met this guy. I am sure it was online, but the overriding memory of his rudeness is so strong, I can't remember much else. I do remember his dancing...but I'll get to that in a minute. There were two dates. Which for me, isn't too bad considering I am the queen one-date wonder.

The first date was just for a drink. We met at Bonefish Grill which I thought was pretty bold considering The Criminal. I recognized him immediately...good sign. I sat down. The first thing out of his mouth was this: *I am so glad you are not skinny.* Seriously? The thought of turning on my heel and heading out the door was more than fleeting. I know what I look like. Actually, I agonize over it, especially before a date. I even tend to avoid mirrors as much as possible. I realize this is a personal problem, but I am pretty sure it does not take a rocket scientist to realize that is not a great opener. He seemed to realize this was not the greatest starter and went overboard to correct. *Um...that's not what I meant...you know....* Okay. This could be a very short date, but we are here. So...get me a freaking drink....

The date was fine. He actually was fairly nice. He was a published composer and had something played on *Saturday Night Live*. Very cool. His day job was singing on a dinner cruise. In the back of my mind, a little debate began...sophisticated musician or cheesy lounge singer....hmmmm. Conversation was good and we seemed to have a few things in common (the arts, appreciation for a nice glass of wine). One weird thing was that every now and then he would just stop what he was saying and kiss me. No warning, no little romantic moment. Very random. Huh. Still not sure how I feel about that.

The next day, he asked me to go to dinner and a movie. He picked me up, smelled overly, and I mean overly, good. While I like a good-smelling guy, breathing is also a plus. But I digress. As we were driving, it became clear that he wanted to demonstrate his singing skills to me, so he blasted the music and started singing at a volume and pitch that should have had the dogs howling. He really wasn't bad, but we were trapped in a small car. At this point I did begin leaning a bit toward cheesy on the cheesy/cool meter. Lucky for me though, short trip to dinner.

BIG RED FLAG

At dinner, we started with decent conversation, but I got a weird vibe pretty quickly. I asked him about kids since he had none. I just wanted a feel for his thoughts or exposure to them since he didn't have any. Did he like kids, had he been around them? This topic of conversation can be a bit of a slippery slope. I never talked too much about my kids in the beginning because I had to decide if I wanted to date the guy. And I never like to get the third degree about the boys because in the beginning they are not relevant. Their existence is, but more than that is too much too fast. So Rude Dude became very serious and very defensive. He seemed to feel like I was attacking him for not having any. I just wanted to know how he felt about kids. I thought it was a normal question. He had this intense stare that kind of backed me up against my seat. I have heard from some people who shall remain nameless that I have a pretty rocking evil eye...but I think Rude Dude has me beat.

Suddenly, after a few minutes, he lightened up and was normal. It happened again when he began to give me his financial situation in a nutshell. Now, this is not something I would ever ask, especially on a first date. It is really an uncomfortable situation to have someone list his assets. I mean, how do you react to that? Applause? Nod and smile? I should have just said, hey buddy, TMI. He was very serious, almost defensive, rattled off the money list with THE STARE in effect and then popped back to jovial and fun.

So again the internal dialog reels. Does he have a mental disorder that involves cycling? Does he have anger issues? Who can really flip an emotional switch in five minutes flat? Questions that boggle the mind. When I started to envision myself as the road runner shooting from one side of the desert to the other to avoid the plummeting anvil (aka THE STARE), I knew that was not good. Does anyone else ever get these kinds of mental pictures? Just curious...but anyway, on to the movie.

After dinner, we got to the movie really early. Apparently, the perfect seat in the theater is of vital importance. We were so early we had to wait in the hall until the theater was cleaned.

While we stood there waiting, he started talking about moving closer to Pensacola and looking for a job here. This was not something he had in the works before me, but something he was doing for me. While flattering, too much too fast and too much pressure. I began to feel my legs wanting to start a slow jog out of the building. This must have been instinct, and I should have trusted it. But he was sweet and enthusiastic. He talked about taking me to see his dinner cruises, going on trips. And then he started to dance. And sing. In the hallway of the theater. Remember Carlton from *Fresh Prince of Bel Air*? This dude was the older white version. Seriously. Could have been a clone. Now, I don't know whether to be entertained because I appreciate a good show tune as much as anyone, but in the hallway it was a bit much even for me. And the meter **screamed** cheesy. At least I got that little debate settled.

Thankfully, the cleaning crew came out and we went in. As we sat for a while all alone, the theater finally started to fill. At the end of the aisle, I noticed two guys, probably early 20's. They were playing rock, scissors, paper. I looked over and realized they were fighting for the end seat and decided to settle it the only way two boys/men can settle a disagreement-- by playing a game with their hands. For some reason that cracked me up. Two grown men playing rock, scissors, paper for a seat. So I asked them if that was what they were doing. "Yep!" Funniest thing I've seen in a while, I told them.

I looked over at rude-boy. He was not happy. This was the beginning of the end. *"Well,"* he said, *"If you are distracted by that, obviously I am not doing enough to keep your attention."* There it was again...THE STARE. At first I thought he was kidding. I must have looked horrified because he backed off and told me it was fine. *"You are just an observer,"* he said. *"Don't worry about it."* I couldn't help looking up for that anvil...

The next thing I knew, the theater was packed and there were two empty seats next to me and one on the other side of him. Three women came up to us and asked if we could scoot down one so that they could sit together. He looked directly at them. *"No. actually, we can't."* I sat there for a minute. Again, I thought he must be kidding. This had to be a joke, right? I mean, come on. But no response. There was that STARE again. Only this time directed at these poor women. I quickly got up and took the empty seat on the other side of him. *"That was very deftly handled,"* he said. What? Thanks, I think, but why should I have to "deftly handle" my date? It was the longest movie of my life. I sat with my hands in my lap trying not to make any sudden movements. I could not wait to get out of there. He got it. I can't really hide much on my face. When he drove me home, he dropped me off quickly and later sent a text that I was closed off and emotionally unavailable.

And he was right. I was.

To him.

Liar Liar Pants on Fire

Category 1: Liar Liar Pants on Fire (this is a deal breaker, but I will add the next category anyway).

Category 2: I am in desperate need of a 12-step program.

When a guy starts off in the Liar Liar Pants on Fire category, he really doesn't need any other category because you have already established a deal breaker. Accept that as fact, and you will save yourself some time.

Liar Liar contacted me online. The same day he started instant messaging me. He was funny, developed a little banter back and forth, and **seemed normal**. We instant messaged for a few days. He had a decent job in some supervisory/ managerial position at some sort of plant. The facts are a little fuzzy, but you get the picture.

On his profile, he had listed his age, height, educational level, and body type, as all profiles require. At one point while messaging with him, I had looked back to see that he had a degree and asked where he finished college.

At this point we need a little mood music of impending doom.....dum, dum, duuuuuuum!!!!

BIG RED FLAG

"Well, I didn't 'technically' finish college. I have about 25 credits to go."

Ok, well, maybe he's in school, so he is "technically" almost done. So I asked. Nope! He was not in school, hadn't been back since he left (more than 15 years ago) and had no plans to return. And twenty-five hours to go is not really even almost...that's two semesters.

Now the point of this little story is less about the fact that he didn't finish school (although as noted in previous posts, I do prefer someone educated) and more about the fact that he lied about it. And the use of the word "technically" is just camouflage for "I'm telling you a lie right this very minute." There is no "technically" about it. You either finished or you didn't. The End.

The question at this point becomes what is a little white lie, is a little white lie okay, and how far do you go to find out the real story. The answer is that it is not about the one small lie, it is the lie that indicates there may be more of those suckers out there. It really only takes one of these dates to figure this out.

Because I was early in the dating experience at this point, brace yourself, I went on the date. I told myself that maybe it wasn't that big of a deal, "technically" he hadn't finished, blah, blah, blah. It was just a little blip on his profile. What I realized is that knowing that he would lie about something so simple and so unnecessary, what else would he lie about? The entire relationship that was all of one date was tainted with wondering if even the simple stories he told were truth. And I started to realize that if I can't take him at his word, then how will I know if he has a business lunch with that woman or if they really have a frequent-banger card at the Motel 6... This is why I decided to write these stories down. So others will not have to learn the hard way.

On another note, the date itself had multiple other red flags. We went to a bar to get a drink to start. Then we went for hibachi, then back to the same bar for another drink. The guy was a fish. I don't think I have ever seen someone drink so much in such a short time. I am pretty sure that if the date hadn't been trumped by the Liar Liar moniker, he would have been undone by the "I am in desperate need of a 12-step program" category. In the end, I didn't want to ride with him. I insisted that he let me drive which was not an easy feat...he was turning into an angry drunk. I drove myself home, let myself in and thought of the **BIG RED FLAG** I ignored.

They are there for a reason, people, let's all remember to use them.

Elizabeth Denham

The Split Personality Guy

Category 1: Multiple personality disorder.
Category 2: Too much too fast syndrome.
Category 3: Those who fail to embrace their own reality.

I met this guy on Facebook. He Friend requested me. I didn't know him, but we had a mutual friend. We didn't communicate at all for a long while. He posted these odd little animated videos that were based on stories he had written. The graphics were very juvenile and the voices sounded robotic. I just figured he was making some point I didn't really get. So, whatever, he was an artist type. Upon further review of his Facebook, he was living in a small town in New York and auditioning for mostly local theater and sometimes bigger things in New York City. He was 46 years old and a massage therapist living with his mother. I will just let that last one go...

I saw a story he published on Facebook about a girl in a bar who began to flirt with him. She even took him to a private area of the bar. He thought she was going to flirt some more and got excited at this prospect. To his utter disappointment, she started trying to sell him Amway. We all know that heart-sinking feeling of realizing a friend is trying to use us for Amway. This is a universally recognized feeling. I thought his story was pretty hilarious. I wrote him a little note on his

Facebook wall telling him I felt his pain and that he should check out my blog.

He read the whole thing and started writing to me about it. He liked it a lot and wanted to keep in touch to talk about writing and what we were both trying to do with it. Cool. I am thinking it will almost be like a little writing club where we can get ideas, etc. One day he asked if he could call, it would be so much easier, he said. Sure, what the heck. He lives in New York. I will never meet him, so why not? He called that night and we talked for a while. He seemed nice, a little intense. He asked if he could call again. The first week or so, he called a lot. I could tell he liked me and was starting the too much too fast syndrome. He wanted to plan to come visit and said he could really see himself liking me. Too much too fast. It's just rampant. I was thinking this was just going to be about writing and it never crossed my mind he would be thinking of visiting. But he is from New York. People say things like that and they never happen. So I wasn't worried.

BIG RED FLAG

One night on the phone, he dropped a little gem. *"I am going to send you a friend request under my real name."*

"Real name? Arthur is not your real name?"

"Arthur is my stage name. My real name is Marco." The mind reels. Stage name? Huh?

"I want you to start getting in the habit of calling me by my real name, Marco, if we continue this."

Well, sheesh. First, continue "this?" "This" sounded like a loaded word the way he said it. What is THIS? And I guess I can try, but when you have seen someone's name on your

Facebook and talked to them on the phone, it is not easy to just shift mid-stream.

"Arthur, I mean Marco."

"Hello? Oh hi, Arthur, I mean Marco."

Ugh.

Not to mention: THAT IS THE WEIRDEST THING I HAVE EVER HEARD!!!!! I don't think **BIG RED FLAG** even begins to describe that a non-famous, local theater actor with odd little animated video stories has a stage name, and multiple Facebook pages, and introduces himself with the stage name. Is it just me? Maybe it is...maybe it is I who has lost perspective on "**normal**." Yeah. No. Pretty sure it's not me. Phew!

And then too much too fast syndrome reared its ugly head. He called and asked me that if I were to date anyone else while he was calling me, would I please not tell him. He tended toward jealousy and he would not handle that well. And he would do the same for me. Well, thanks, I guess. But at that point, I started hoping he would happen upon the girl of his dreams in New York. Immediately. And should I have told him I was actually dating someone...kind of? Nah...he already told me not to...

At some point during our little...what do I call it? Not a relationship, obviously. Not really a friendship because the whole split personality thing precluded me from knowing either Arthur or Marco well enough to call "Friend." How about experience? That'll work. So at some point he seemed to recognize that he was a bit intense with the calls and the jealousy.

BIG RED FLAG

"I need to take a step back," he said. *"I know I can be overwhelming."*

I always get so excited for a glimmer of self-awareness.

"What if I just call you once a week...I will call you every Thursday around 9."

Nothing like being locked in to a weekly phone date, but okay. Better than four nights a week and emails on top of that. We will try that. I find myself thinking at this very moment, why? Why did I agree to a weekly phone date? Already there were many Red Flags...multiple names, self-expressed jealousy, too intense, living with this mother (see, I couldn't just leave that one alone). It is a mystery. I should have just said "no thanks."

But we had our weekly phone date. Once. The second week was near my birthday. I was busy that week and tired and just didn't feel like talking on the phone. So when he called, I didn't answer. He called twice in a row and left messages. I was just too tired to talk...well, to him... The next morning I texted him that I was tired and so sorry I missed his phone calls.

No response.

Oh well. I am not sure how long it took me, at least a week, to notice that I hadn't heard from Arthur/Marco. I checked my Facebook and lo and behold, they had both deleted me! Can you believe it? I couldn't resist sending a little message to find out why I deserved so harsh a punishment. And here is what I sent:

"I was a little surprised to find myself no longer your friend. I hope the best for you."

Here is what Arthur sent back (verbatim) (and pay attention, he switches personas with reckless abandon, so it's hard to keep up):

Actions speak louder than words. You're actions of not returning my phone call spoke volumes. You're very nice and lovely woman, but I wasn't really feeling it. Maybe I ask too Thanks for wishing me your best. Actions speak louder than words. You're actions of not returning my phone call spoke volumes. You're very nice and lovely woman, but I wasn't really feeling it. Maybe I ask too much, but I don't really think i do. Thanks for wishing me your best

If you care, it shows.
If you care, it shows.

And here is what Arthur sent two minutes later (verbatim):

Actions speak louder than words. You're actions of not returning my phone call spoke volumes to me. It said Your just *NOT* that into me(or at least not equally) I have no room or patience for that anymore.

You're very nice and lovely woman, but I wasn't really feeling it. I think I would overwhelm you. Maybe I ask too much, but I don't really think i do. I just know what works for me and what does *NOT*. Thanks for wishing me your best I wish you the same. Hope you find someone who *YOU* are equally into as *THEY* are into you. -Marco-...

(I swear, that is verbatim. Marco signed Arthur's FB messae.)

And here is what Marco sent one minute after that:

Actions speak louder than words. You're actions of not returning my phone call spoke volumes to me. It said Your just *NOT* that into me(or at least not equally) I have no room or patience for that anymore. You're very nice and lovely woman, but I wasn't really feeling it. I think I would overwhelm you. Maybe I ask too much, but I don't really think i do. I just know what works for me and what does *NOT*. Thanks for wishing me your best I wish you the same. Hope you find someone who *YOU* are equally into as *THEY* are into you. -Marco-..

(And this time, Marco signed his own...)

I guess he just needed me to be clear that they both felt that way and that I shouldn't contact either of them again.

Bummer.

It could have been like two for the price of one...

Elizabeth Denham

The Effeminate Guy

I had a date. He was a little effeminate. The End.

The Wanna Feel My Muscle Guy

Category 1: Those who fail to embrace their own reality.

Category 2: Those who think that women can't keep their hands off of them.

This was yet another one-date wonder. I'm sure you can guess why from the title. He was a former body builder turned podiatrist. That, in itself, is chuckle worthy. His profile talked a good bit about his body building days. I am sure he was very proud of his overly large physique. He must have been since he had pictures on his profile of his competitions. You know, the typical enormous, muscle-bound, greased and posed body emerging from the tiny Speedo. To his credit, he also had recent pictures of his less-than-muscle-bound, older and thicker self.

I am not big on overly-big, body builder type guys. I like an athletic guy who is strong and manly, but there can be too much of a good thing. The reason I decided to go out with him was because in his profile, he talked about his family and his work. In emails and on the phone, he mentioned helping to take care of his aging parents and talked about how, as a podiatrist, he worked mostly with older patients. He seemed genuinely sweet and smart, and these are the qualities you look for in a guy.

We met for dinner at a seafood place near me. He lived about an hour away, so I appreciated that he was willing to drive to my neighborhood for dinner. When we arrived and met in the parking lot, he looked like his photo (and was big, but not overly-so, and much shorter than he listed in his profile), was polite and greeted me with a hug. I think the hug thing was more significant than I realized in the beginning. More on that at the end of the date.

The restaurant was near the water, but had no real view. The atmosphere was casual, yet offered white linen tablecloths and candlelight. It is a typical mix of the low-key, good food combination for which Pensacola is known.

We sat down to dinner, ordered drinks and I was about to embark on the typical first-date small talk. Before I could open my mouth, he looked up from the menu and said,

"Wanna feel my muscle?"

Really? What does that mean? That question is just wrong on more than one level. That is hilarious. He is funny. These are my immediate thoughts as I almost fell out of my chair laughing under the impression that he was joking. In the midst of my hysteria, I looked up and he was not laughing. He looked a little perplexed at my response. It hit me that he was not joking. I'm pretty sure he actually thought I would want to feel his muscle.

Before I could recover my composure, he asked,

"Wanna feel my hair?"

Okay. Now I have no idea how to respond, especially since he stuck his head out toward me a little. I kind of gently patted him on the head and said something like, "Very nice."

He looked a little disappointed. I felt a bit bad, but I still don't know what the appropriate response should have been. Should I have felt his muscle (ugh) and his hair (double ugh)

and ooohed and ahhed over his immense strength? I don't think I could have mustered the sincerity to have that be believable. Should I have just said, "You are joking, right?" I may have bruised his ego even more. It seemed to genuinely surprise him that I didn't jump at the chance to get my hands on him. Maybe my response did him a favor and introduced the possibility that every woman does not want to cop a feel on the first date.

We made it through dinner…and dessert. The conversation was somewhat forced; my fault I am sure, since I deflated him within the first five minutes. He walked me to my car where he hugged me goodbye. And hugged me and hugged me and hugged me. I think the purpose of the hug was to determine what kind of shape I was in more than anything. He kept pulling me closer and standing back and repeating the process. It was apparent and disturbing to me that I was being analyzed. I thanked him, got in my car and The End. I guess I didn't pass muster. Either that or he had the self-awareness to realize that I didn't really get him. Because I never heard from him for a second date.

Until…stay tuned for Guys Who Forgot They Had a Date With You.

The Parking Lot Guy (Update)

I received an email from Parking Lot Guy not long ago (but about a year after the parking lot meowing episode). It boggles the mind that after facing rejection the first time around, some of these men come back for more, and I am forced into yet another "update" entry. I have a theory about that to be addressed in the next chapter. Here is the email:

elizabeth in pensacola

ebeth,

so no hot make out dates in walmart parking lot lately? u must be working too hard. If ur looking for a volunteer, then look no farther. have willing mouth for you and can travel.

Name withheld to protect the drunk?

If he was sober when he wrote that I will eat my hat.

Let's dissect this interesting email. First of all, *"ebeth?"* Two dates, the second of which ended with meowing while trying to make out in a parking lot, does not elevate us to nickname status. I have never been a girl to have shortened my name, and after multiple emails (in which I signed my full name every time) and two dates, Mr. Meow obviously didn't pick up on that little quirk of mine. Not really shocking considering the arrival of this latest email, is it?

Second, I really dislike emails that are written in texting short-hand. Considering I correct my sons' texts when they misspell or use text short-hand, I really don't love it for texting either. And do I even need to mention the use of "farther?" I know the farther/further distinction is a toughie, but picking the wrong one is like nails on a chalkboard.

Mini-Break for a Grammar Lesson

Farther: Shows a relation to physical distance. If you can replace the word farther with "more miles" then that is correct.

• We drove farther than I thought we would on a tank of gas.

• He wanted to run farther, but his legs hurt.

• My house is farther from the beach than yours.

Further: Relates to metaphorical distance or depth. It is a time, degree or quantity.

• There needs to be further discussion on that issue.

• I need to look further into the details of the plan to build the house.

Since I am not looking miles and miles to make out with someone in a parking lot, it is more of a metaphorical search. Mr. Meow should have used "further."

Moving on…

Last, *"have willing mouth for you and can travel?"* Ewww! My first thought upon reading that line was, "What does that even mean?" It sent a shiver down my spine…and not in a good way. I'm not sure how that offer is supposed to be appealing. Does he mean he will travel to a parking lot near me? And he wants to make out? Or does he want to talk? Nah. Or maybe he just needs to sing me a ditty. Since the parking lot theme has come up twice, three times if you count this email, I am beginning to wonder if I have some sort of vibe that elicits this kind of invitation from men. If so, someone please help!!

I let Mr. Meow off the hook and did not respond to the email. I decided to color him drunk (it's the only way I can wrap my mind around it) and call it a day!

The Teeth Licker

Category 1: Just plain weird.

Category 2: Those who just need an audience.

Category 3: Those who want to get married and you will do.

Dating Tips:

1. *If you don't like his kiss, The End. You don't want to end up with someone whose kiss you dread.*
2. *If you can put the phone down, take a shower, come back and he hasn't stopped talking to know you were gone, he is not interested in you.*
3. *If you are not interested, tell him the minute you realize it.*
4. *If you have to give yourself the "benefit of the doubt" speech, get out now.*

This was a guy with whom I had been acquainted in the distant past. I remembered him as a nice, funny person with a bit of a dorky side. He had a gregarious personality and could move from group to group with ease. I hadn't seen him in years. We bumped into each other and as he (and apparently I, heehee) looked exactly the same from 15 years ago, we recognized each other instantly. We realized that we were both living in town and were both divorced.

Under the guise of catching up, he asked to meet me for lunch. It was one of those moments when you aren't sure if you are meeting an old friend to reminisce or you are on a date. This can be a touchy situation and happens more than one might think. Do you dress up? Do you let him pay? Do you laugh at all his jokes? Or in my case, laugh when it isn't a joke (remember Wanna Feel My Muscle Guy). So many ifs! If he is interested and you are not...embarrassing! If you are interested and he is not...embarrassing! Risk Factor is HIGH!

The general rule of thumb is to be prepared for either, unless you are adamantly opposed to the date part. If you are opposed to the date part, you MUST pay for yourself. It's only right. If you are interested, you are going to have to wing it and try to feel him out to see where his intentions lie.

Our lunch was nice. We went to a little downtown restaurant that is located in an old historic house. It served things like quiche, salads and sushi. We didn't lack for conversation at all. Having even a remote history with someone makes a date so much easier. We talked about mutual friends and what they were all doing these days. We talked about what we had been doing for the last decade. We talked about our kids and life as parents, since the last time we saw each other we were kids ourselves. He was funny and had story after story to tell (this becomes significant in the not-too-distant future). Easy peasy. After lunch, I was still unsure about the definition of our outing. He made no moves, and I paid for myself. We got in our cars and that was that.

BIG RED FLAG

Later that week he called. The cloud began to lift. He wanted to "get together" again. Okay. Pretty sure it was a DATE! We couldn't plan anything for more than a week as the coming weekend was both of our kid weekends. During that week, he called daily. At this point I was sure of the interest level, but a daily call that soon is pretty red flaggish. I like communication, and daily contact can be a great way to make you feel good. At first I enjoyed the attention and the fact that he could carry on a conversation. He was filled with stories and made me laugh.

The problem: Too much of a good thing.

The daily calls would last forever. Inevitably, he called near bedtime for my kids. I would try to do the bedtime routine while talking to him and then would hang up to get them in bed. He usually was in the middle of a "story" and it was hard to find a stopping point to get off the phone. I began to realize that the act of him going from the front door to the car could result in a story of gargantuan proportions. When you start to roll your eyes at the realization of the onset of a new (and ever-so-mundane story), you know it is not good! A few times, I did put the phone down to say goodnight to a child. I figured I would say we were cut off and call him back if he discovered my conspicuous absence. Never happened. Not once. I could say goodnight to the boys, come back, and he would still be talking.

Now let's talk about how that makes one feel. The fact that you are actually not needed as a participator in the conversation, but merely to provide an audience, causes your value in the relationship--whether two days or two years--to plummet. If it takes two years to recognize it, then we need to talk. The point is, there is no interest in who you are, what you need, or what you can offer other than your listening ability.

At any rate, we had already planned another date, so I went. The thing was, I liked him as a person. He was a good guy and a good dad. He was honest and genuinely nice. I tried to give myself the overused "benefit of the doubt" speech. You know the one: "It's so hard to find a decent guy, I can overlook these things. They are minor and I can get over them." If you find you are self-administering that speech, STOP.

BIG RED FLAG

At the end of the date, he walked me to the door and kissed me. As I had fully bought into my own "benefit of the doubt" speech, I let him. Words can't really describe what ensued, but I will try my best. He licked my teeth. And not the fronts of them--more the tops of the molars as if his tongue were a toothbrush. Back and forth, back and forth. Any time you start to think of ANYTHING other than the fact that you are enjoying a kiss, you should never kiss that person again.

And all I could think was this, "What are you doing? Are you seriously licking my teeth? Stop!!"

He stopped to talk for a minute (read: tell a very long and less-than-riveting story). While he was talking, I began another benefit-of-the-doubt speech to myself. It probably was a fluke. Maybe I misunderstood this kiss. I know, what does that even mean? But I just couldn't imagine that he did it on purpose. So when he went for kiss number two, I didn't reject him. Big mistake. As you were probably thinking, there is no way to misunderstand a kiss. I realize that now. Lesson learned.

The next day I sent him an email stating that I just didn't feel the romantic feelings one should feel in a dating relationship. I thought we were just great friends. His response: *I completely agree.* Phew!!!

Three months later, he was engaged to someone else. Huh. Anyone will do? Anyone who will listen, I guess.

The Guys Who Forgot They Had a Date/Conversation With You

Category 1: The Self-Absorbed.

Category 2: Those who are too busy telling you how great they are to notice how great you are.

Category 3: Those who want a date and you will do.

Dating Tips:

1. *There is zero excuse for someone forgetting that they spoke to you online, much less that they went on an actual date with you. Do not dignify this with a response.*

It seems crazy to me that I even have to write an entry with this title. Even though I participated in online dating for years, I never forgot someone to whom I spoke or someone with whom I had a date. I don't think this is unusual. I think most people put some degree of thought into who they contact, who they email and in whom they are interested. Evidently, some online daters do not. I guess they are haphazardly contacting people and hoping someone responds. And I guess when you contact people based on volume, not genuine interest, you forget when you have communicated with some of them. And let me tell you, when it happens to you, it is definitely an insult. It is one of those times when the "we are just not a good fit" mentality is difficult to apply. I mean, how would they even know if you are a good fit because they evidently didn't even pay close enough attention to you the first time around?

Let's start with Wanna Feel My Muscle Guy. I never heard from him after our awkward and disturbing prolonged hug-at-the-end date. I thought this was great. No need to gracefully exit. No disappointment that either of us liked the other more. It was just done. Yea! And then, about eight or nine months later, I got an email through the dating site. *"I really like your profile and would love to get to know you."* He went on to tell me a little bit about his family, his aging parents and his podiatric practice.

I didn't even have to think about this one. I knew immediately who he was. Because really, how could I forget the guy who wanted me to feel his muscle? The dilemma is this: Do you let him off the hook and not tell him that he went on an actual date with you or do you tell him and let him squirm? I think the answer is obvious. I did try to be nice about it.

"Hi there, I just wanted to let you know that we already had a date…at Landry's in Pensacola about eight months ago. But thank you for contacting me."

"Hey! I thought that was you! Just making sure. How are you? What have you been up to?"

Now, at least he had the backbone to write back. And I guess he attempted to cover his mistake well. No guy who "thought that was you" writes an email as if they have never spoken to you if they do, in fact, remember you. Just doesn't happen. Following my theory that once you have said what you have to say, you are not obligated to continue communicating, I did not write back.

As for the ones who email and forget that they have emailed, I made a surprising discovery! And I don't know why I was surprised. I guess it was because I tried to write emails that were specific to the person to whom I was writing. It is not easy to write someone you don't know, but I would read the profile and try to pull something from it that I thought was nice or interesting and weave it into the conversation. What happens with the forgetful is that they write a boilerplate email and send it to anyone they might like. After all, copying and pasting is so easy and efficient. Why would you want to invest any time into something as silly as finding someone to date? This tactic would definitely make it harder to remember if you have already contacted someone, especially if there was not much communication involved. My solution to this fun event was to copy and paste the (identical) email they had sent previously and send it back. Typically I would get no response from this, but occasionally I would get, *"Oh, sorry."*

I also want to address my theory on the guys with "Updates" in this book. It goes to the same idea as the guys who forget you. Well, kind of. In the world of online dating, if you do it long enough, you start to see the same people over and over again. Unless you are in a big city, the pool of those who are in your demographic is somewhat limited.

So while these dates may have been creepy or weird, I think that when there is a dry spell, people tend to think time and distance might dull the memory of the creepy and weird.

That is...if they remember you...

The Old Guy

Category 1: Those who fail to embrace their own reality.

Category 2: Those who are too busy telling you how great they are to notice how great you are.

Category 3: Master of the backhanded compliment.

Dating Tips:

1. When your instincts tell you to delete someone, trust them.

BIG RED FLAG

The old guy.

Doesn't that say it all? At the time he wrote to me, I was probably 36 years old. He was 67. Yep, you read it right. 67. There is no legitimate reason for someone 31 years your senior to write to you. I should have deleted the email immediately based solely on that fact, but I was curious. Older men had written to me before, but 31 years older? What was he thinking? I had to know. This line of thinking has been my downfall…or maybe offered me the opportunity to experience these bizarre stories (remember the same thought in my mind during Parking Lot Meow Guy?). Curiosity killed the cat…or made for a funny story…

I was teaching ballet at that time and had mentioned it in my profile. He wrote a long email telling me that he was a ballroom dance teacher and would like to teach me. At that point, I went back to re-read his profile.

BIG RED FLAG

He was retired. He was successful. He was handsome. He was a pilot who owned a private plane and travelled the world. He entered and won many ballroom dance competitions. The handsome comment required further inspection of his photos. There was one. It was extremely grainy and from what I could make out "one foot in the grave" popped to mind, and waaaaay older than 67.

Now here's the thing about a bragging kind of profile. It screams insecurity or arrogance or both. Either quality is unattractive. The other thing is that if you write a profile like that, you have to make it believable. The old guy lived in Foley, Alabama. Foley is typical small-town Alabama, kind of a one-stoplight-town. It was a stretch for me to believe that someone who was as this profile described would live in Foley, Alabama. And every time I have had a niggling doubt about the veracity of a profile, I have been right. It goes to trusting your instincts. Always trust your instincts.

His email went on to say that ballroom is the most romantic form of dance that exists. It is great exercise and everyone should do it. He believed that most Americans were lazy "couch potatoes" and could use some culture. He figured that I must be in somewhat decent shape (see the backhanded compliment?) since I taught ballet, but his big question was

"Can you really dance?" Oh, and by the way, he added, and I will quote this since it is too good to gloss over: *"While I may be biologically 67, I have been medically tested and I am physiologically 37, and you would be lucky to keep up."*

Can you imagine the rate at which my mind was spinning? Where to even begin? So many declarations. Ballroom is a romantic form of dance, but as a ballet teacher, I do believe I am entitled to my own opinion. Is it just me? As far as most Americans being uncultured, lazy couch potatoes, I am not a big fan of gross (insulting) generalizations, particularly since it felt like he was trying to find out the status of my health and cultural intelligence.

Typically, if I failed to delete an obviously deletable email, I would at least have the good sense not to respond. In this case, good sense abandoned me in my bafflement over his logic. Physiologically 37? Really? He couldn't be serious. This was my call to respond.

I decided to address the only thing that really mattered in all of his blather. His age. I told him that as wonderful as it must be to be physiologically 37, I was more concerned with the fact that he was biologically 67. He was older than my father and well out of my age-range. I added that dating him was not something I was interested in.

He wrote back. When someone has a profile touting their many accomplishments, they almost always write back. The arrogant ones need to be right and can't fathom that you would reject them in all of their glory. The insecure ones need to know what they did wrong. Response to either just feeds these needs and is never a good idea. I obviously didn't follow my own rules on this one.

He said I was "myopic" in not being able to see the difference between his biological and physiological ages. That is my favorite insult of all time. When was the last time anyone called you myopic? Outstanding word!

He further stated that I "inferred" in my profile that I could dance and that I didn't answer his question. "Can you really dance?" And then, the unthinkable happened. He corrected my grammar. He said, "By the way, you left a preposition dangling when you said 'dating you is not something I am interested in.' "

Big sigh. This is not something I can let go. I must answer, AGAIN against my better judgment. What is wrong with me? I know this is wrong. And yet I can't stop! Help!

My Response

"I am still not interested, myopic or not. You are too old for me or anyone my age, especially since I have three young boys. You would be lucky to keep up with them. Furthermore, when I email with people, I write conversationally. And I would never have the gall to correct the grammar of a total stranger. Since you corrected mine, I will just remind you that the writer implies, and the reader infers."

And with that, I deleted him.

The Republican

Category 1: The One.

Dating Tips:

1. Sometimes going with instinct and breaking the rules works.

When I read this guy's profile, it made me think. He had a whole Venn Diagram theory about men being blue and women being pink and the overlapping interests were purple. His idea was that you had to find the person with whom you had the most purple. Okay. This made sense and math isn't really my thing, so I just went with it. I liked the fact that he had put some thought into what he wanted to say. He was articulate, he was educated and his family was important to him. So far, so good, right? But I had been in the position of optimism before only to be asked to Sweeten the Deal. So I was never without a "we shall see" attitude.

At this point, the only negative was that he was a Republican from Alabama (if you think the Florida Panhandle is red, try the whole of Alabama!). My sister thought this was enough to be a deal breaker. I wasn't convinced. We emailed a few times before he called. He had a deep voice and a

Southern accent. He asked questions, listened and made me laugh. After we talked, he sent me an email with a list of activities and asked me to word associate with each one. The list included things like theater (love it), wine (a necessity of life), sunset cruise (never done it but sounds fun), live music (like, but not if I want to talk to someone), movies (again, like, but not if I want to talk to someone), etc. Did he put this kind of thought into all of his dates? Huh.

The next time we talked, he asked if I would like to try the sunset cruise. This little invitation went against my "no water date" rule; but he said there would be a boat captain, so I made an exception. In planning the date, he asked to pick me up, but would meet me if I were more comfortable. He had to drive from Alabama to Pensacola (1 hour) to Destin (another hour). I never let anyone pick me up, but the more we talked and the more planning we did, it was just easier and I had a very comfortable feeling with him. I let him pick me up and broke another of my rules for dating.

He picked me up on a Saturday afternoon. I opened the door and was pleasantly surprised. His online picture was attractive, but in person he was even better. I remember telling him later in the date that he needed a better picture because the one he was using didn't do him justice. Of course, then I thought, "Why would I say that? I hope he takes it as a compliment and not a lack of interest!"

Conversation flowed easily on the drive and we stopped at a local fish market to get food and wine for the cruise. He was gracious, opening doors, letting me pick the food and wine, not letting me carry anything. In fact, when we got to the dock, he wouldn't let me carry anything at all. He looked like a pack mule carrying my bag and the groceries. He said, *"I have two girls, I am used to being a pack mule."*

The cruise was beautiful. The Gulf Coast emerald green waters sparkling, dolphins swimming around us and the warm August breeze keeping us from being too hot. Our captain was a funny surfer-dude-lived-on-the-water-my-whole-life type of guy who was probably in his 50's. When Donald got up to go the restroom at one point, the captain asked if this was our first date. When I confirmed it, he said, "Impressive," in his Southern surfer drawl. It was impressive.

Throughout the cruise, we had good conversation. We talked about our families and our kids. He asked more about my online dating. I forgot to mention that I had broken yet another of my dating rules when I told him of this book (that was still a blog) before we even met. It goes back to the theory of scare tactic or screening tool. He was not intimidated and didn't really understand why any normal guy would be. To me this is a sign that a guy doesn't relate to any of the before-referenced issues in dating. And I was right.

After the cruise, we went to the bar at the dock to have the dessert we had been too busy talking to eat. We had our dessert and a beer and proceeded to walk along the boardwalk. He held my hand as we walked down and back. As we neared the parking lot, he stopped to lean down to kiss me. It was sweet and soft and not too much. As I was thinking about this, he bent down and said, *"Are we in a parking lot?"*

I looked around and we were on the edge of one. Laughter ensued. As the breeze had diminished and it was getting late, we headed back to the car. I was getting a little tired, but I wasn't ready for the date to end. Odd for me, I know. Usually I couldn't figure a way out fast enough. When we got to my house, wait for it.....I invited him in! The biggest and final rule broken. I don't know what it was, but Donald evoked a feeling of calm in me from the beginning. He seemed to provide information voluntarily and easily. He had nothing to hide and was intent on making me feel comfortable. We sat on the couch and talked, and before I knew it, I had rested my head on his shoulder. As I fell asleep, we lay together comfortably. It felt like home. We dozed for a couple of hours before he left. I told him that I know it probably didn't feel that way, but the fact that I fell asleep on him was a very good thing. I hadn't slept well in years. It felt like home and I never looked back.

Donald's Perspective

Donald wrote to one of his good friends the day after our first date to give him a post-date analysis. Here is what he wrote:

It is 11:30 Sunday morning, and the fact that I have already been to church, grabbed breakfast and a spark plug for my lawnmower, does not lead one to believe that last night's date belongs on the Dream Team. I got home shortly before 2 am, and at 7:15 this morning, my racing mind would not give way to sleep anymore. Picture me standing on the podium, gold medal hanging from the ribbon around my neck.

First, let's back up and get a little info on Elizabeth Reosti. I give you her last name because I think you need to read her blog (entitled "you can't make this sh*t up") about online dating to begin to get an idea of the fascinating compilation that she is. I told her she is a statistical anomaly, that there is no probability model which can accurately depict her experiences with online dating. Only the psychos are subjects for her writing and she has given each a nickname.

184

The subject line above is the nickname I thought of for myself as I drove home early this morning. It is taken from something she said last night on two occasions, and is borrowed from the 400 lb guy she went out with that one of her friends dubbed "Big Fat Date". I think the Roman numerals add a certain stateliness.

Before we went out, I asked her in our initial phone conversation what she enjoyed doing, and she replied that she really was happy doing most anything. This was a sincere statement, but I decided to dig a little deeper. The next day I sent her an email entitled "Word Association" and asked her to respond to the words in my list with the first thought that came into her head. Here is a sampling of the list

* *Food Allergies*

* *Favorite food*

* *Waterfront Dining*

* *Live Music*

* *Sunset Cruise*

* *Theatre*

* *Wine*

She embraced it. For Sunset Cruise, she responded "love the idea, never been on one". For wine she put "a necessity of life". I also had a fill in the blank question-

185

* _____ *is something I would like to do if I had someone fun to go with.*

She mentioned that her Sunday School class had a social each month, and they alternated between events with kids and without. She said she never attended the adult only events because it was not much fun being the only single at the event. She qualified that with "I know this isn't a dating type thing, but it is the first thing that came to mind."

She concluded the email by saying, "great list . . . that was fun. Do you always put this much into planning dates?"

Enter stage left Captain Brian and his 33' Catamaran harbored in Destin. Sunset cruise starts at 6 and you get back to the harbor around 8. Go out into the gulf and see some dolphins (around the jetties where you, Rob, and I snorkeled once upon a time). Sail back through the pass and go into the bay and watch the sunset while you eat and/or drink. Charge is per hour and the boat holds 3 to 6. Guess what? No others were scheduled, so we had the boat to ourselves. And you know what? It was a full moon. And guess what? There was a nice breeze. Captain Brian moved in and out of the conversation adroitly, and then encouraged us to get out on the trampoline, the canvas stretched between the pontoons at the bow, when we hit the calm waters of the bay.

At one point in the conversation I told her I had a theory about her rash of bad experiences. She took her long brown hair and moved it behind the shoulder that was farthest away from me, tucked her chin down towards her collarbone in an

186

alluring way that defies description, and said, "You do? Let's hear it." I opened with, "You disarm men." She tilted her head to the side and looked at me out of the corner of one eye and said, "What do you mean?" I explained that she had a very unique way of making them feel completely at ease and they drop the guise and show their true colors quickly. There is more to this theory, but I stopped at that to be first date appropriate. She thoughtfully considered it and said, "So I weed them out quickly and it is a good thing?" I smiled and said "Exactly".

One bottle of pinot grigio and some assorted deli foods we picked up along way were consumed by the time we motored back to the dock. As we walked up the dock to climb the stairs and sit on the empty balcony outside the restaurant to get a drink and finish our dessert at Captain Brian's behest, she said, "Thank you, this has been the Best First Date (BFD) I have ever had." I took her beach bag to the car, walked into the restaurant to get us a beer and water at the bar, and delivered the drinks to the table where she was sitting. I needed to complete Brian's tip from the bill I broke at the bar and walked down to the boat. When I was walking back on the dock I looked up to the balcony and saw her turned in her chair looking under the balcony rail to watch me walk towards her. File that as noteworthy, I thought. When I sat at the table my noteworthiness was validated. She said, "You should add some pictures to your profile - you are much more attractive in person. Not that you are not attractive in your picture. It is a compliment. Maybe it is better that way, because it is a pleasant surprise."

We finished and walked along the boardwalk, but neither was in the mood to stop and listen to music and the breeze was nowhere to be found. As we ran out of boardwalk, we turned to walk back to the car and we had our first kiss. We drove to her house (1 hour) and two hours later, I headed to the car to leave. At the door, she repeated "Best First Date ever".

I will be traveling to Destin on Thursday for a meeting. I called Elizabeth a few minutes ago to talk for a quick conversation and see if she is available Thursday evening for dinner on my way back. Date 2 is on the calendar.

After the Tommy John surgery of the last year or so, I might have added a few more mph to my once feared heater - throwing effortlessly now and with no pain.

The object of your vicarious single guy dreams, DD

Could you ask for better than that? And with such a stellar first date, I had to marry the guy! We got married 11 months after our first date. We have five kids between us. The boys and I moved to Alabama and they have transitioned easily. We have the same ups and downs and problems as anyone else. But we also have an enduring love because we learned from our experiences and defined what is important to us both in our lives. The trials of divorce and post-divorce dating can teach you either to become angry and bitter and untrusting or they can teach you to know what you want and not to settle for anything less. I waited seven years for "The One."

And it was worth every single crazy, bad, hilarious moment of dating.

BIG RED FLAGS

1. Guys who ask absolutely no questions about you. This is a great indicator of self-absorption. It will always be all about them

2. Guys who assume you have nothing better to do than await their calls. These are the last-minute planners. They think that you couldn't possibly have anyone else interested in you and you are waiting by the phone. Insulting and arrogant.

3. Guys who say they never drink or drink daily. Either is a sign of a problem. Never drinking shows that they have had to quit drinking too much or they are very religious. The daily drinker has no real responsibility or doesn't care. Neither is good for those of us who enjoy a glass of wine at the end of a long day.

4. The recently divorced or, even worse, separated. These are often users of the description "it's complicated." Do not listen when they say they are ready to date. Statistically, not a good risk.

5. Guys who tell you how great they are. Show me, don't tell me.

6. Guys who tell you how much money they have. This is a version of too much too soon, and relegates you to being perceived as having money as a top priority.

7. Guys who want your life story on the first date. Another version of too much too soon designed to put you on the spot. It is often a test to see how "open" you are. Don't buy it. You don't owe your most personal story to a complete stranger. A guy who respects you will wait until you offer it. He will not force you into it.

8. Guys who don't have a photo on their online profiles. First of all, fair is fair. I posted mine, you post yours. Second, this makes me nervous. It begs the question, are you not who you say you are? Are you someone I know who is playing a trick on me, my ex-husband, ex-boyfriend, a nutty friend? Not comforting. Not okay.

9. Guys who tell you they look different from their photo before you meet. Guys talk a ton about women who don't look like their photos. And with good reason. No one wants to be shocked upon seeing you. And personally, I wouldn't want to be greeted with a look of shock upon being seen. Nothing good can come from this, and it is tantamount to a lie.

10.   Guys who tell you what they lost in the divorce. They are not past anger or bitterness and should be relegated to the category of those not ready to date.

11.   Guys who use pseudonyms. I really don't need to explain this one, do I?

12.   Guys who use words like "technically" and "actually" a lot. This means they are not committed to absolute truth.

13.   Guys who are 15-20 years older or younger. These men have a motive. They will not be able to relate to your kids, and why add further pressure to an already challenging situation…second marriage, blended families.

14.   Guys who mention information about you that you have not shared. While you may research someone and they may research you, it's creepy and weird to leak information found on the internet. A guy should at least give you the courtesy of letting him know you.

15. **Guys who you don't like kissing.** This is a deal breaker. If you do not like kissing someone, it is not something you can live without. You have to be attracted to and want to kiss the person you are with. Period.

16. **Guys who call you daily right off the bat.** This is too much too fast. It puts pressure and expectations on you immediately. This should evolve naturally.

17. **Guys who tell you they need to "step back" before a relationship has even begun.** Thankfully, this guy has self-awareness. Trust him on this one.

18. **Guys who are rude to you or to other people on a first date (or second or third or ever).** If this is their best first-date behavior, it only goes downhill from here. Run.

19. **Guys who think that parking lots are appropriate first-date destinations.** This needs no explanation.

20. **Guys who meow.** This also needs no explanation.

21. **Guys who are on their first date since their divorce.** If it is also your first date, you are fine. If not, you don't need to be someone's dating practice.

22. **Guys who say, "My wife, I mean ex-wife."** They obviously have not embraced their own reality and are not ready to date.

23. **Guys who set expectations before you even meet.** For example, expecting a certain texting or calling frequency is premature. Expecting you to account for your time to him is also premature. And controlling. Run.

24. **Guys who want to take you on trips before they have even met you.** This shows an insecurity that they think they will overcome by going over the top. It also shows a lack of awareness of how this would make most women feel.

I don't know many women who would take a trip with a perfect stranger.

25.   Guys who think a first date involving guns of any kind is appropriate. Enough said.

26.   Guys who insult women in their profiles. That is too big of a mountain to climb.

27.   Guys who use the word "future" on a first date. This would fall into the too much too fast category.

28.   Guys who never move past email communication. These guys are one of several possibilities: insecure, hiding something, not really interested in dating or bored. None is a good option.

29.   **Guys who try too hard.**   They are either insecure or feel they have something to prove. You will spend a lot of time trying to convince them that you know how great they are. This is a job, not a relationship.

Dating Tips

1. "Can you still have kids?" is not a first-date question.
2. If you say you will call, call. This goes for men and women. We are not in high school anymore.
3. If you are not interested, say so. This goes for men and women. The alternative of making someone wonder is just plain cruel. As I said, we are not in high school anymore.

> a. Example: Thank you so much for the nice dinner. I just don't think we are a good fit. [See how this makes it not personal? No criticism, no list of faults. Easy peasy.]

4. To save time, all of these tips apply to both men and women.
5. Don't have a dramatic buildup to a non-dramatic story. It just sets up immediate disappointment. And, you look like a drama queen.
6. Don't email too long with an online date if you are truly ready to date. If you find yourself lingering in the world of email or text, either you don't really want to go out with the person, or you are avoiding real dating altogether. Take your own hint.
7. Follow your own rules. No excuses. Who needs regret?
8. No guy wants to "watch a movie at my house." This is innuendo. Believe me.
9. Have a friend who knows your date's name and where you are going. This means that you, too, must know his name – first and last.

10. Give your date's phone number to a friend before your first date. This means you must also have his phone number.

11. Meet an online date in a public place with which you are familiar.

12. Lunch-hour dates are a good idea.

13. Don't go to someone's house who you don't know. I shouldn't have to say this, but it happens.

14. Do not go to the beach, river, lake or any other body of water with a first date. Too easy to hide the body.

15. Do not ride in a boat on any of the above mentioned bodies of water. Again, too easy to hide the body.

16. When writing your online profile, do not indicate who you do NOT want to respond to your profile. It's just negative.

17. If someone lives far, far away, just say no. It is never as easy to start off long-distance dating as you convince yourself it is. Just don't go there.

18. If someone toots his own horn, it's probably because no one else is tooting it.

19. If someone sets expectations before you meet, run far, far away.

20. Beware of too much too fast. Your friends know you are great, but a total stranger doesn't know you well enough to know that. I could be a nut. You have no idea after 15 minutes.

21. Beware of poor-pitiful-me syndrome. Trying to be with someone who is hell-bent on feeling sorry for himself is a no-win situation.

22. If a guy says, "My wife, I mean ex-wife," clearly, he is not ready to date.

23. Don't invite your date (a total stranger) to an event with your friends. There are several problems with this. First, it is hard to form your own opinion as friends can never keep theirs to themselves. Second, too much pressure. Third, you can't get to know someone in a group. Too much attention shifting.

24. Secrets must be earned by the evolution of a relationship. They should not be revealed out of obligation or pressure from your date.

25. "I am not dating anyone else." Words that need to be said before exclusivity can be assumed. Do the words, "I never said this was exclusive" ring a bell to anyone?

26. Do not respond to a profile with no photo unless the guy is willing to email one immediately. No conversation should take place until this happens. You don't want to wonder why there is no photo or doubt the veracity of the profile.

27. Do not feel obligated to respond to every single wink, email, or contact from an online dater. In many cases, it is obvious that you are not a match and if it isn't obvious to him, well, BIG RED FLAG. Self-awareness is key.

28. When your instincts tell you to delete someone, trust them.

29. If an online dater has only one photo and it is from the shoulders up, be prepared for anything.

30. Don't ride in a car with someone on a first date.

31. Pay attention to a date's actions. If the actions do not match the words, this becomes a **BIG RED FLAG.**

32. **BIG RED FLAGS** are there for a reason. Use them.

33. Look to date a fully formed person, not a work in progress.

34. You don't get to make someone account for their time after the first date. And this goes both ways.

35. When telling someone you don't want to date, do not give a list of what is wrong with them. Just because they are not right for you, does not mean they are not perfect for someone else.

36. Once you have said what you have to say, you are not obligated to continue communicating. Avoid dragging the end out. It's kinder.

37. If you have to give yourself the "benefit of the doubt" speech, walk away. Your instincts are almost always right.

38. If you don't like his kiss, the end.

39. You are allowed to be freaked out by those who exhibit freaky behavior.

40. If you are still angry at your last (or any) significant other, do not write an online dating profile.

41. If you are still angry at your last (or any) significant other, do not ask your friends to set you up.

42. If you are still angry at your last (or any) significant other, do not date at all.

43. If you think you are past your anger, and you do get online and find yourself listing all of the things that you do not want, then turn the computer off immediately.

44. If you think you are past your anger and find yourself online to date and write a nice profile, but are thinking of all the things you don't want with someone in your past in mind...try again later.

45. If you think you are past your anger, have some degree of optimism that there are decent people in the world, then give it a go.

46. If someone says: Well, I am leaving you a voicemail, so either you are busy or avoiding my calls. [This one is designed to make you feel guilt whether you have done something wrong or not. Run.]

47. If someone says: Your actions speak that you are not as into me as I am into you. I don't have time or room for that in my life. [Run. You will probably never be able to feed that kind of need.]

48. If someone says: I just don't think I am good enough for you (or, in the reverse, you are too good for me). [This one is designed to elicit a speech from you touting the enormous...and it better be enormous... list of stellar attributes that you love about him/her. And then you must spend time convincing him/her that it is, in fact, true. Run. You will be making lists until the end of time.]

49. If someone says: I think you like so-and-so better than you like me. [The best answer to this is a simple, "yes." Less work than running and definitely less work than the convincing game this manipulator is trying to make you play.]

50. If someone says: You never respond to my texts; I guess you aren't thinking about me during your day. [Run like hell. You will never convince this person that you might actually be BUSY even though you might be busy and thinking of him/her and just can't take time to tell him/her. You know, working, taking care of kids. This is called the case of the self-absorbed.]

51. If someone judges your whole gender negatively, you are already starting off in a hole; don't try to dig your way out of the flaws of half the world. Move on.

52. Appreciate people for who they are – even if they are just not right for you.

53. If someone drunk texts you before or after a first date, run. Where do you have to go from here?

54. If a profile has no smiling photo, beware of missing teeth.

55. Don't assume a potential date has nothing better to do than wait on you to call for a last-minute date. It is rude, arrogant and assumes you are more important than you are.

56. Repeat this – and mean it: I would rather be alone for the rest of my life than be with the wrong person.

57. Repeat this – and mean it: *A deal breaker should actually break the deal.*

Categories of Dates

1. Those who aren't ready to date.
2. Those who were never ready to date.
3. The guys your dad warned you about.
4. The self-absorbed.
5. The cynical ones.
6. Too much too fast.
7. His way or the highway.
8. Those who fail to embrace their own reality.
9. Those who DO possess self-awareness.
10. Those who are too busy telling you how great they are to notice how great you are.
11. Those who can't be alone and you will do.
12. Those who just want to get married and you will do.
13. Liar liar pants on fire.
14. Those who are in desperate need of a 12-step program.
15. The great omission (really a subset of liar liar pants on fire).
16. People who think they are sensitive, but really they are just dumbasses.
17. Those who are too insecure to date.
18. Those who should just keep their own company.
19. Those who just aren't right for you.
20. Those who think their profiles are witty and cute, but really they are not.
21. Just plain weird.
22. I love you, but I've never met you.
23. Poor pitiful me.

24. Those who do not learn from others' mistakes.
25. Those who do not take "no" for an answer.
26. The ones who kind of freak you out.
27. The effeminate ones.
28. Master of the backhanded compliment.
29. Those who leave your mouth agape with their rudeness.
30. Those who think saying "technically" is a sufficient cover for the fact that they are about to lie.
31. Those who think women can't keep their hands off of them.
32. Guys who forgot they had a date/conversed online with you.
33. Those who just need an audience and the anatomical presence of your ears renders you qualified.
34. The One.

What They Really Mean AKA Online Decoder

1. Statement: I want someone active. Definition: No fatties need apply.
2. Statement: I want an "independent" woman. Definition: I don't want to support you.
3. Statement: Technically (using this word ever in a profile or email or any form of communication whatsoever). Definition: What follows is a lie.
4. Statement: I don't drink. Definition: I have a drinking problem.
5. Statement: I drink daily. Definition: I have a drinking problem.
6. Statement: It's complicated. Definition: I am too weak to make a decision and I want my cake and eat it too.
7. Statement: Well, I am leaving you a voicemail, so either you are busy or avoiding my calls. Definition: You should feel guilty for not answering the phone whether you have done something wrong or not.
8. Statement: Your actions speak that you are not as into me as I am into you. I don't have time for that in my life. Definition: I am needy. Run. You will probably never be able to fill this kind of need.
9. Statement: I just don't think I am good enough for you (or, in the reverse, you are too good for me). Definition: I need you to shower me with reassurance. This is designed to elicit a speech from you touting the enormous...and it better be enormous...list of stellar attributes that you love

about him/her. And then you must spend time convincing him/her that it is, in fact, true. Run. You will be making lists until the end of time.

10. Statement: I think you like so-and-so better than me. Definition: I am needy. The best response to this is a simple "yes." Less work than running and definitely less work than the convincing game this manipulator is trying to make you play.

11. Statement: You never respond to my texts; I guess you aren't thinking about me during your day. Definition: I am needy. Run like hell. You will never convince this person that you might actually be BUSY even though you might be busy and thinking of him/her and just can't stop to say so. You know, working, taking care of kids. This is the case of the self-absorbed.

Afterward

It took me a long time to find my happy ending.

During the years after my divorce, I didn't date, dated, took breaks, dated again and at times felt discouraged. And now, looking back, I believe that I met my husband when I was ready to meet him. I was willing and ready to be alone for the rest of my life rather than be with the wrong person. So often in life, you have to go through an evolution before you are ready for someone else. Having self-awareness during that process is difficult, but necessary.

I hope that my journey has helped you to understand that we all evolve at our own pace, that rejection does not indicate that there is something wrong with you but that you just weren't right together. I hope you have recognized that because someone isn't for you, doesn't mean there isn't a perfect person out there for him – and for you. And most importantly, I hope you learned that your deal breakers must actually break your deal.

All of this is to say, you must value yourself, know who you are and know what you want. You are entitled to standards, to happiness and to love. I am so glad that I did online dating and stuck with it. I am so glad for the lessons I learned and the men in this book, especially The Republican who has supported me in writing my story. What is life without stories? What is life without experience?

And what is life without hope?

Elizabeth

About the Author

Elizabeth Denham is a freelance commercial writer and author. She lives in Spanish Fort with her husband and their five children (three came with her and two came with him). Like most mothers, she has no free time, but when she neglects her other responsibilities, she spends time working on her next book and blogging about life with her blended family.

Links:
sweetenthedeal.com
elizabethdenhamwrites.com
http://www.huffingtonpost.com/elizabeth-denham/